Appetizers
Starters &
Hors d'oeuvres

The Ultimate Collection of Recipes
to Start a Meal in Style

Appetizers Starters & Hors d'oeuvres

The Ultimate Collection of Recipes to Start a Meal in Style

Consultant Editor:

Christine Ingram

Select Editions

Produced for distribution by Select Publications
8036 Enterprise Street, Burnaby, BC V5A 1V7, Canada
Ph: (604) 415-2444 Fax: (604) 415-3444

This edition published in 2001 by Select Editions

A CIP catalogue record for this book is available from the British Library

ISBN 1 894722 65 5

Publisher: Joanna Lorenz
Editor: Charlotte Berman
Designer: Bill Mason
Jacket Designer: Mark Latter
Illustrator: Anna Koska
Editorial Reader: Diane Ashmore
Recipes: Catherine Atkinson, Alex Barker, Steve Baxter, Angela Boggiano, Carla Capalbo, Kit Chan, Jacqueline Clarke,
Maxine Clarke, Andi Cleverly, Roz Denny, Joanne Farrow, Rafi Fernandez, Silvano Franco, Christine France, Sarah Gates,
Shirley Gill, Nicola Graimes, Rosamund Grant, Carole Handslip, Deh-Ta Hsing, Peter Jordan, Elisabeth Lambert Ortiz,
Ruby Le Bois, Clare Lewis, Sara Lewis, Leslie Mackley, Norma MacMillan, Sally Mansfield, Sue Maggs, Sallie Morris, Jenny Stacey,
Liz Trigg, Hilaire Walden, Laura Washburn, Steven Wheeler, Kate Whitman, Elizabeth Wolfe-Cohen, Jeni Wright
Photography: Karl Adamson, Edward Allwright, Steve Baxter, James Duncan, John Freeman, Ian Garlick, Michelle Garrett,
Peter Henley, John Heseltine, Janine Hosegood, Amanda Heywood, David Jordan, Maris Kelly, Dave King, Don Last,
William Lingwood, Patrick McLeavy, Michael Michaels, Thomas Odulate, Sam Stowell

Printed and bound in Singapore

1 3 5 7 9 10 8 6 4 2

CONTENTS

Introduction

For many people starters are the best part of a meal. Indeed, they are so popular, that sometimes whole dinner parties consist entirely of a variety of starters. You can see the attraction – starters by definition mean small portions, which means there can be a huge and delicious selection of different dishes. Of course for the cook, providing such a medley of diverse foods can be quite a challenge, (although one you may well feel equal to) but for the guests it will be nothing less than a complete delight!

In some countries, "starters" have become an institution. Tapas, in Spain, are a meal in their own right, and the Italians' antipasto is so varied and delicious that you'd be forgiven for wishing to stop right there with the artichokes and superb dried hams, and forget entirely about the pasta and meat that follow.

The list of different starters is almost endless. If you're planning a sophisticated dinner party, it is possible to start with a simple but tasty appetizer such as Marinated Olives or Pork and Peanut Wontons with Plum Sauce which can be served easily beforehand with drinks. Your choice of starter should take its cue from the food you intend to serve as a main course. You need to choose this with care, as the starter will set the tone for the rest of the meal. Select something fairly light, such as Grilled King Prawns or a simple salad if you plan to serve a roast meat or hearty stew. If, on the other hand, you are barbecuing fish or grilling chicken, you could decide on something more elaborate. Vegetable or fish terrines look pretty and taste wonderful, or choose from one of the many special occasion starters. For an Oriental meal, you could make a Thai-style soup, or serve Chicken Satay with Peanut Sauce. However, don't feel too constrained by the ethnicity of your meal. Today, the trend is to serve foods that complement each other. A Mediterranean-style starter such as Charred Artichokes with Lemon Oil Dip could happily come before an Indonesian green curry. Similarly, Malayan Prawn Laksa would be fine before a French or Italian-style meal. Those rules that do exist are concerned with texture and taste. For example, if you're making a soufflé or roulade as a main course, choose something crunchy as a starter.

There is something for every occasion in this book, and whether it's soups or nibbles, party food or family favourites, you are bound to be inspired to start a meal in the best possible way.

Garnishes

Many garnishes are delicate works of art which seem almost a shame to eat, and others add a dash of texture or a hint of colour without which the dish would just not be the same.

CREAM SWIRL

Pour a swirl of cream, soured cream or yogurt to make a bowl of soup look particularly attractive.

To create a delicate pattern draw the tip of a fine skewer back and forth through the swirl.

CROÛTONS

Croutons are an easy and effective way to use up stale bread whilst adding crunch to any dish, and are always served with gazpacho and Caesar salad.

1 Once you have cut your chosen bread into small cubes either fry them in sunflower oil until they are golden and crisp, or brush them with oil and bake in the oven. They will keep in an airtight container for up to a week.

CUCUMBER FLOWERS

This is a stunning garnish which would grace any dinner party.

1 Cut the cucumber in half lengthways and remove the seeds. Place each half cut-side down and then cut at an angle into 7.5cm/3in lengths. Cut into fine slices stopping 5mm/¼in short of the far side, so that the slices remain attached.

2 Fan the slices out. Turn in alternate slices to form a loop. Bend the length into a semicircle so the cucumber loops resemble the petals of a flower.

LEMON TWIST

A classic garnish – so simple but very effective.

Cut a lemon into 5mm/¼in slices. Make a cut in each slice from the centre to the skin. Hold the slice either side of the cut and twist to form an "S" shape.

PARMESAN CURLS

Curls of Parmesan add a delicate touch to pasta or risotto.

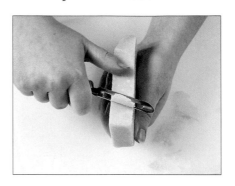

Holding a swivel-bladed peeler at a 45° angle, draw it steadily across the block of Parmesan cheese to form a curl.

CHILLI FLOWERS

Make these chilli flowers several hours before needed to allow the "flowers" to open up.

1 Use a small pair of scissors or a slim-bladed knife to cut a chilli carefully lengthways up from the tip to within 1cm/½in of the stem end. Repeat this at regular intervals around the chilli – more cuts will produce more petals. Repeat with the remaining chillies.

2 Rinse the chillies in cold water and remove all the seeds. Place the chillies in a bowl of iced water and chill for at least 4 hours. For very curly flowers leave the chillies overnight.

CHIVE BRAIDS

Try floating a couple of edible braids of chives in a bowl of soup.

1 Align three chives on a worksurface with a bowl on one end to hold them still. Carefully plait the chives together to within 2.5cm/1in of the end.

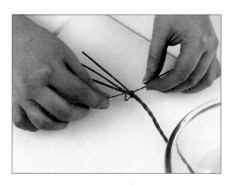

2 Tie a thin chive around the exposed end of the plait. Remove the bowl and tie the other end the same way. Trim both ends with kitchen scissors.

3 Plaice the braid in a bowl and pour boiling water over them. Leave to stand for 20–30 seconds then drain and refresh under cold water. Drain again.

SPRING ONION TASSELS

You can often find this garnish in Chinese restaurants, where the appearance of a dish is almost as important as its taste.

Cut the white part of a spring onion into a 6cm/2½in length. Shred one end of each piece, then place in iced water for about 30 minutes until the ends curl.

TOMATO SUNS

Colourful cherry tomato suns look good with pâtés and terrines.

1 Place a tomato stem-side down. Cut lightly into the skin across the top, edging the knife down towards the base on either side. Repeat until the skin has been cut into eight separate segments, joined at the base.

2 Slide the top of the knife under the point of each segment and ease the skin away towards the base. Gently fold the petals back to mimic the sun's rays.

AVOCADO FAN

Avocados are amazingly versatile – they can serve as edible containers, be sliced or diced in a salad, or form the foundation of a delicious soup or sauce. They also make very elegant garnishes.

1 Halve, stone and peel an avocado. Slice each half lengthways into quarters. Gently draw a cannelle knife across the quarters at 1cm/½in intervals, to create regular stripes.

2 Make four cuts lengthways down each avocado quarter leaving 1cm/½in intact at the end. Carefully fan out the slices and arrange on a plate.

Marinades, Oils and Dressings

Marinades, flavoured oils and dressings can turn a plain piece of fish or a sliced vegetable into a delectable appetizer, starter or hors d'oeuvre. With a few simple ingredients, and in just a few minutes, you can make a fresh herb marinade to tenderize fish or meat , a ginger and garlic oil for fragrant fried dishes, or a soured cream dressing to bring out the flavour of crisp salad vegetables.

SUMMER HERB MARINADE

Make the best of summer herbs in this marinade. Any combination may be used depending on what you have to hand, and it works well with veal, chicken, pork or lamb.

1 Discard any coarse stalks or damaged leaves from a selection of herb sprigs, such as chervil, thyme, parsley, sage, chives, rosemary and oregano, then chop finely.

2 Mix the herbs with 90ml/ 6 tbsp olive oil, 45ml/3 tbsp tarragon vinegar, 1 garlic clove, crushed, 2 spring onions, chopped, and salt and pepper. Add the meat or poultry, cover and chill for 2–3 hours

GINGER AND LIME MARINADE

This refreshing marinade is particularly good with chicken.

1 Mix together the rind of one lime and the juice of three limes. Add 15ml/1 tbsp green cardamom seeds, crushed, 1 finely chopped onion, grated fresh root ginger (use a 2.5cm/1in piece and peel before grating), 1 large garlic clove, crushed and 45ml/3 tbsp olive oil.

2 Pour over the meat or fish. Stir gently to coat, cover and leave in a cool place for 2–3 hours.

CHILLI AND GARLIC MARINADE

Add extra chillies if you like your food to be very spicy.

1 Combine 4 small chillies, seeded and finely diced, 10ml/2 tsp finely grated fresh root ginger, 1 large garlic clove, crushed, and 45ml/3 tbsp light soy sauce in a bowl. Add the meat or fish, cover and chill for 2– 4 hours.

CHINESE MARINADE

This marinade is traditionally used to flavour succulent duck breasts.

1 Mix 15ml/1 tbsp clear honey, 1.5ml/1¼ tsp five spice powder, 1 garlic clove, finely chopped, 15ml/1 tbsp hoisin sauce and a pinch of salt and pepper. Add the duck breasts or other meat, turning them in the marinade. Cover and leave in a cool place to marinate for 2 hours.

AROMATIC SPICE OIL

As well as tasting delicious, aromatic oils make wonderful gifts. Ginger Garlic and Shallot Oil is simple and delicious, but you could also try using a combination of other spices and flavourings, such as chillies, coriander, lemongrass, peppercorns and lime leaves.

1 Peel and lightly bruise a 6cm/2½in piece of fresh root ginger and place in a clean bottle. Fill with groundnut oil, 2 garlic cloves (left whole) and 3 small peeled shallots. Cover tightly and leave in a cool dark place for 2 weeks, or until the flavour is sufficiently pronounced, before using.

PARSLEY, SAGE AND THYME OIL

Chop a handful each of fresh parsley, sage and thyme. Place in a bottle and fill up with olive oil. Seal and allow to stand at room temperature for about a week, shaking occasionally. Strain the oil into another sterilized, decorative bottle, discard the chopped herbs but add a fresh sprig or two to decorate.

SOURED CREAM AND DILL DRESSING

This unusual dressing can be made in only a couple of minutes.

1 Blend together 120ml/ 4fl oz/½ cup soured cream, 10ml/2 tsp creamed horseradish and 15ml/1 tbsp chopped fresh dill in a small bowl and season with a little salt and pepper.

SPICY TOMATO DRESSING

This tangy dressing goes very well with a robust salad, such as bean or potato salad. It can also be used as a marinade.

1 Mix together 5ml/1 tsp ground cumin, 15ml/1 tbsp tomato ketchup, 30ml/2 tbsp olive oil, 15ml/1 tbsp white wine vinegar and 1 garlic clove, crushed in a small bowl. Add a little salt and some hot pepper sauce to taste and stir again thoroughly.

HERB GARDEN DRESSING

The dried mixture will keep throughout the winter until your herbs are growing again. It can also be used to sprinkle over vegetables, casseroles and stews.

1 Mix together 115g/4oz/1 cup dried oregano, 115g/4oz/1 cup dried basil, 50g/2oz/½ cup dried marjoram, 50g/2oz/½ cup dried dill weed, 50g/2oz/½ cup dried mint leaves, 50g/2oz/½ cup onion powder, 30ml/2 tbsp dry mustard, 10ml/2 tsp salt and 15ml/1 tbsp freshly ground black pepper and keep in a sealed jar to use as needed.

2 When making a batch of salad dressing, take 2 tbsp of the herb mixture and add it to 350ml/12fl oz/1½ cups of extra virgin olive oil and 120ml/4fl oz/ ½ cup cider vinegar. Mix thoroughly and allow to stand for 1 hour or so. Mix again before using.

NIBBLES
AND DIPS

Marinated Olives

For the best flavour, marinate the olives for at least 10 days and serve at room temperature.

INGREDIENTS

Serves 4

225g/8oz/1⅓ cups unpitted, green olives

3 garlic cloves

5ml/1 tsp coriander seeds

2 small red chillies

2–3 thick slices of lemon, cut into pieces

1 thyme or rosemary sprig

75ml/5 tbsp white wine vinegar

1 Spread out the olives and garlic on a chopping board. Using a rolling pin, crack and flatten them slightly.

2 Crack the coriander seeds in a mortar with a pestle.

3 Mix the olives and the garlic, coriander seeds, chillies, lemon pieces, herb sprigs and white wine vinegar in a large bowl. Toss well, then transfer the mixture to a clean glass jar. Pour in cold water to cover. Store in the fridge for at least 5 days before serving at room temperature.

> ### COOK'S TIP
> ⌣
>
> For a change, use a mix of caraway and cumin seeds in place of the coriander.

Salted Almonds

These crunchy salted nuts are at their best when fresh so, if you can, cook them on the day you plan to eat them.

INGREDIENTS

Serves 2–4

175g/6oz/1 cup whole almonds in
  their skins

15ml/1 tbsp egg white, lightly beaten

2.5ml/½ tsp coarse sea salt

> ### COOK'S TIP
> ⌣
>
> This traditional method of salt-roasting nuts gives a matt, dry-looking finish; if you want them to shine, turn the roasted nuts into a bowl, add 15ml/1 tbsp of olive oil and shake well to coat.

1 Preheat the oven to 180°C/ 350°F/Gas 4. Spread out the almonds on a baking sheet and roast for about 20 minutes, until cracked and golden.

2 Mix the egg white and salt in a bowl, add the almonds and shake well to coat.

3 Turn out on to the baking sheet, give a shake to separate the nuts, then return them to the oven for 5 minutes, until they have dried. Set aside until cold, then store in an airtight container until ready to serve.

Potato Skins with Cajun Dip

Divinely crisp and naughty, these potato skins are great on their own or served with this piquant dip as a garnish or on the side.

INGREDIENTS

Serves 4

2 large baking potatoes

vegetable oil, for deep-frying

For the dip

120ml/4fl oz/½ cup natural yogurt

1 garlic clove, crushed

5ml/1 tsp tomato purée or

   2.5ml/½ tsp green chilli purée or

   ½ small green chilli, chopped

1.5ml/¼ tsp celery salt

salt and ground black pepper

1 Preheat the oven to 180°C/350°F/Gas 4. Bake the potatoes for 45–50 minutes until tender. Cut them in half and scoop out the flesh, leaving a thin layer on the skins. Keep the flesh for another meal. Cut the potatoes in half once more.

2 To make the dip, mix together all the ingredients and chill.

3 Heat a 1cm/½in layer of oil in a saucepan or deep-fat fryer. Fry the potatoes until crisp and golden on both sides. Drain on kitchen paper, then sprinkle with salt and black pepper. Serve the potato skins with a bowl of dip or a dollop of dip in each skin.

Celeriac Fritters with Mustard Dip

The combination of the hot, crispy fritters and cold mustard dip is extremely good.

INGREDIENTS

Serves 4

1 egg

115g/4oz/1½ cups ground almonds

45ml/3 tbsp freshly grated Parmesan cheese

45ml/3 tbsp chopped fresh parsley

1 celeriac, about 450g/1lb

lemon juice

oil, for deep-frying

salt and ground black pepper

sea salt flakes, to garnish

For the dip

150ml/¼ pint/⅔ cup soured cream

15–30ml/1–2 tbsp wholegrain mustard

1 Beat the egg well and pour into a shallow dish. Mix together the almonds, grated Parmesan and parsley in a separate dish. Season with salt and plenty of ground black pepper. Set aside.

2 Peel and cut the celeriac into batons about 1cm/½in wide and 5cm/2in long. Drop them immediately into a bowl of water with a little lemon juice added to prevent discoloration.

3 Heat the oil to 180°C/350°F. Drain and then pat dry half the celeriac batons. Dip them into the beaten egg, then into the ground almond mixture, making sure that the pieces are coated completely and evenly.

4 Deep-fry the fritters, in batches, for 2–3 minutes until golden. Drain on kitchen paper. Keep warm while you cook the remaining fritters.

5 Make the dip. Mix the soured cream, mustard and salt to taste. Spoon into a serving bowl. Sprinkle the fritters with sea salt.

Chilli Bean Dip

This deliciously spicy and creamy bean dip is best served warm with triangles of grilled pitta bread or a bowl of crunchy tortilla chips.

INGREDIENTS

Serves 4

2 garlic cloves

1 onion

2 green chillies

30ml/2 tbsp vegetable oil

5–10ml/1–2 tsp hot chilli powder

400g/14oz can kidney beans

75g/3oz mature Cheddar cheese, grated

1 red chilli, seeded

salt and ground black pepper

3 Drain the kidney beans, reserving the liquor. Blend all but 30ml/2 tbsp of the beans to a purée in a food processor.

6 Cut the red chilli into tiny strips. Spoon the dip into four individual serving bowls and scatter the chilli strips over the top. Serve warm.

1 Finely chop the garlic and onion. Seed and finely chop the green chillies.

4 Add the puréed beans to the pan with 30–45ml/2–3 tbsp of the reserved liquor. Heat gently, stirring to mix well.

2 Heat the vegetable oil in a large sauté pan or deep frying pan and add the garlic, onion, green chillies and chilli powder. Cook gently for about 5 minutes, stirring regularly, until the onions are softened and transparent, but not browned.

5 Stir in the whole beans and the Cheddar cheese. Cook gently for about 2–3 minutes, stirring until the cheese melts. Add salt and pepper to taste.

COOK'S TIP

For a dip with a coarser texture, do not purée the beans; instead mash them with a potato masher.

Lemon and Coconut Dhal Dip

A warm spicy dish, this can be served either as a dip with warmed pitta bread or as an accompaniment to cold meats.

INGREDIENTS

Serves 8

5cm/2in piece fresh root ginger
1 onion
2 garlic cloves
2 small red chillies, seeded
30ml/2 tbsp sunflower oil
5ml/1 tsp cumin seeds
150g/5oz/⅔ cup red lentils
250ml/8fl oz/1 cup water
15ml/1 tbsp hot curry paste
200ml/7fl oz/scant 1 cup coconut cream
juice of 1 lemon
handful of fresh coriander leaves
25g/1oz/¼ cup flaked almonds
salt and ground black pepper

2 Heat the sunflower oil in a large, shallow saucepan. Add the ginger, onion, garlic, chillies and cumin. Cook for about 5 minutes, until the onion is softened but not coloured.

4 Stir in all but 30ml/2 tbsp of the coconut cream. Bring to the boil and cook, uncovered, for a further 15–20 minutes, until the mixture is thick and pulpy. Off the heat, stir in the lemon juice and coriander leaves. Season to taste.

3 Stir the lentils, water and curry paste into the pan. Bring to the boil, cover and cook gently over a low heat for about 15–20 minutes, stirring occasionally, until the lentils are just tender and not yet broken up.

5 Heat a large frying pan and cook the flaked almonds for one or two minutes on each side until golden brown. Stir about three-quarters of the toasted almonds into the dhal.

1 Use a vegetable peeler to peel the ginger and finely chop it with the onion, garlic and chillies.

6 Transfer the dhal to a serving bowl; swirl in the remaining coconut cream. Scatter the reserved almonds on top and serve warm.

VARIATION

Try making this dhal with yellow split peas: they take longer to cook and a little extra water has to be added but the result is equally tasty.

Hummus Bi Tahina

Blending chick-peas with garlic and oil creates a surprisingly creamy purée that is delicious as part of a Turkish-style mezze, or as a dip with vegetables. Leftovers make a good sandwich filler.

INGREDIENTS

Serves 4–6

150g/5oz/¾ cup dried chick-peas

juice of 2 lemons

2 garlic cloves, sliced

30ml/2 tbsp olive oil

pinch of cayenne pepper

150ml/¼ pint/⅔ cup tahini paste

salt and ground black pepper

extra olive oil and cayenne pepper,
  for sprinkling

flat leaf parsley sprigs, to garnish

1 Put the chick-peas in a bowl with plenty of cold water and leave to soak overnight.

2 Drain the chick-peas, place in a saucepan and cover with fresh water. Bring to the boil and boil rapidly for 10 minutes. Reduce the heat and simmer gently for about 1 hour until soft. Drain in a colander.

3 Process the chick-peas in a food processor to a smooth purée. Add the lemon juice, garlic, olive oil, cayenne pepper and tahini paste and blend until creamy, scraping the mixture down from the sides of the bowl.

4 Season the purée with plenty of salt and ground black pepper and transfer to a serving dish. Sprinkle with a little olive oil and cayenne pepper, and serve garnished with a few parsley sprigs.

COOK'S TIP

For convenience, canned chick-peas can be used instead. Allow two 400g/14oz cans and drain them thoroughly. Tahini paste can now be purchased from most good supermarkets or health food shops.

Baba Ganoush with Lebanese Flatbread

Baba Ganoush is a delectable aubergine dip from the Middle East. Tahini – a sesame seed paste with cumin – is the main flavouring, giving a subtle hint of spice.

INGREDIENTS

Serves 6

2 small aubergines

1 garlic clove, crushed

60ml/4 tbsp tahini

25g/1oz/¼ cup ground almonds

juice of ½ lemon

2.5ml/½ tsp ground cumin

30ml/2 tbsp fresh mint leaves

30ml/2 tbsp olive oil

salt and ground black pepper

For the flatbread

4 pitta breads

45ml/3 tbsp sesame seeds

45ml/3 tbsp fresh thyme leaves

45ml/3 tbsp poppy seeds

150ml/¼ pint/⅔ cup olive oil

1 Start by making the Lebanese flatbread. Split the pitta breads through the middle and carefully open them out. Mix the sesame seeds, chopped thyme and poppy seeds in a mortar. Work them lightly with a pestle to release the flavour.

2 Stir in the olive oil. Spread the mixture over the cut sides of the pitta bread. Grill until golden brown and crisp. When cool, break into pieces and set aside.

3 Grill the aubergines, turning them frequently, until the skin is blackened and blistered. Remove the peel, chop the flesh roughly and leave to drain in a colander.

4 Squeeze out as much liquid from the aubergine as possible. Place the flesh in a blender or food processor, then add the garlic, tahini, ground almonds, lemon juice and cumin, with salt to taste. Process to a smooth paste, then roughly chop half the mint and stir into the dip.

5 Spoon the paste into a bowl, scatter the remaining mint leaves on top and drizzle with the olive oil. Serve with the Lebanese flatbread.

Basil and Lemon Dip

This lovely dip is based on fresh mayonnaise flavoured with lemon juice and two types of basil. Serve with crispy potato wedges for a delicious starter.

INGREDIENTS

Serves 4

2 large egg yolks

15ml/1 tbsp lemon juice

150ml/¼ pint/⅔ cup olive oil

150ml/¼ pint/⅔ cup sunflower oil

4 garlic cloves

handful of fresh green basil

handful of fresh opal basil

salt and ground black pepper

1 Place the egg yolks and lemon juice in a blender or food processor and process them briefly until lightly blended.

2 In a jug, stir together the oils. With the machine running, pour in the oil very slowly, a little at a time.

3 Once half of the oil has been added, the remaining oil can be incorporated more quickly. Continue processing to form a thick, creamy mayonnaise.

4 Peel and crush the garlic cloves. Alternatively, place them on a chopping board and sprinkle with salt, then flatten them with the heel of a heavy-bladed knife and chop the flesh. Flatten the garlic again to make a coarse purée.

COOK'S TIP

Make sure all the ingredients are at room temperature before you start to help prevent the mixture from curdling.

---

5 Tear both types of basil into small pieces and then stir into the mayonnaise along with the crushed garlic.

6 Add salt and pepper to taste, then transfer the dip to a serving dish. Cover and chill until ready to serve.

Thai Tempeh Cakes with Dipping Sauce

Made from soya beans, tempeh is similar to tofu but has a nuttier taste. Here, it is combined with a fragrant blend of lemon grass, coriander and ginger, and formed into small patties.

INGREDIENTS

Makes 8 cakes

1 lemon grass stalk, outer leaves removed, finely chopped

2 garlic cloves, finely chopped

2 spring onions, finely chopped

2 shallots, finely chopped

2 chillies, seeded and finely chopped

2.5cm/1 in piece fresh root ginger, finely chopped

60ml/4 tbsp chopped fresh coriander, plus extra to garnish

250g/9oz/2¼ cups tempeh, defrosted if frozen, sliced

15ml/1 tbsp lime juice

5ml/1 tsp caster sugar

45ml/3 tbsp plain flour

1 large egg, lightly beaten

vegetable oil, for frying

salt and freshly ground black pepper

For the dipping sauce

45ml/3 tbsp mirin

45ml/3 tbsp white wine vinegar

2 spring onions, finely sliced

15ml/1 tbsp sugar

2 chillies, finely chopped

30ml/2 tbsp chopped fresh coriander

large pinch of salt

1 To make the dipping sauce, mix together the mirin, vinegar, spring onions, sugar, chillies, coriander and salt in a small bowl and set aside.

2 Place the lemon grass, garlic, spring onions, shallots, chillies, ginger and coriander in a food processor or blender, then process to a coarse paste. Add the tempeh, lime juice and sugar, then blend until combined. Add the flour and egg, and season well. Process again until the mixture forms a coarse, sticky paste.

3 Take a heaped serving-spoonful of the tempeh paste mixture at a time and form into rounds with your hands. The mixture will be quite sticky.

4 Heat enough oil to cover the base of a large frying pan. Fry the tempeh cakes for 5–6 minutes, turning once, until golden. Drain on kitchen paper and serve warm with the dipping sauce, garnished with chopped fresh coriander.

Guacamole

Avocados discolour quickly so make this sauce just before serving. If you do need to keep it for any length of time, cover the surface of the sauce with clear film and chill in the fridge.

Serves 6

2 large ripe avocados

2 red chillies, seeded

1 garlic clove

1 shallot

20ml/2 tbsp olive oil,
   plus extra to serve

juice of 1 lemon

salt and ground black pepper

flat-leaf parsley leaves, to garnish

1 Halve the avocados, remove the stones and scoop out the flesh into a large bowl.

2 Using a fork or potato masher, mash the avocado flesh until smooth.

3 Finely chop the chillies, garlic and shallot, then stir into the mashed avocado with the olive oil and lemon juice. Season to taste.

4 Spoon the mixture into a small serving bowl. Drizzle over a little olive oil and scatter with a few flat-leaf parsley leaves. Serve immediately.

Quail's Eggs with Herbs and Dips

For al fresco *eating or informal entertaining this platter of contrasting tastes and textures is delicious and certainly encourages a relaxed atmosphere. Choose the best seasonal vegetables and substitute for what is available.*

INGREDIENTS

Serves 6

1 large Italian focaccia or 2–3 Indian
    parathas or other flatbread
high quality olive oil, plus extra to serve
1 large garlic clove, finely chopped
small handful of chopped fresh mixed
    herbs, such as coriander, mint, parsley
    and oregano
18–24 quail's eggs
30ml/2 tbsp home-made mayonnaise
30ml/2 tbsp thick soured cream
5ml/1 tsp chopped capers
5ml/1 tsp finely chopped shallot
salt and ground black pepper
225g/8oz fresh beetroot, cooked in water
    or cider, peeled and sliced
½ bunch spring onions, trimmed and
    roughly chopped
60ml/4 tbsp red onion or tamarind and
    date chutney
coarse sea salt and mixed ground
    peppercorns, to serve

1 Preheat the oven to 190°C/
375°F/Gas 5. Brush the
focaccia or flatbread liberally with
oil, sprinkle with garlic, your
choice of herbs and seasoning and
bake for 10–15 minutes, or until
golden. Keep warm.

2 Put the quail's eggs into a
saucepan of cold water, bring
to the boil and boil for 5 minutes.
Arrange in a serving dish. Peel the
eggs if you wish or leave guests to
do their own.

3 To make the dip, combine the
mayonnaise, soured cream,
capers, shallot and seasoning.

4 To serve, cut the bread into
wedges and serve with dishes
of the quail's eggs, mayonnaise dip,
beetroot, spring onion and
chutney. Serve with tiny bowls of
the coarse salt, ground peppercorns
and olive oil for dipping.

COOK'S TIP

If you don't have time to make
your own mayonnaise use the
best shop-bought variety
available. You will probably find
that you need to add less
seasoning to it.

Tzatziki

Serve this classic Greek dip with toasted small pitta breads.

INGREDIENTS

Serves 4

1 mini cucumber

4 spring onions

1 garlic clove

200ml/7fl oz/scant 1 cup Greek-style
   natural yogurt

45ml/3 tbsp chopped fresh mint

fresh mint sprig, to garnish (optional)

salt and ground black pepper

1 Trim the ends from the mini cucumber, then cut it into 5mm/¼in dice.

2 Trim the spring onions and garlic, then chop both very finely.

COOK'S TIP

Choose Greek-style yogurt for this dip – it has a higher fat content than most yogurts, which gives it a deliciously rich, creamy texture.

3 In a glass bowl, beat the yogurt until completely smooth, if necessary, then gently stir in the chopped cucumber, onions, garlic and mint.

4 Add salt and plenty of freshly ground black pepper to taste. Transfer the mixture to a serving bowl. Chill until ready to serve; garnish with mint if liked.

Parmesan Fish Goujons

Use this batter, with or without the cheese, whenever you feel brave enough to fry fish. This is light and crisp, just like authentic fish-and-chip shop batter.

INGREDIENTS

Serves 4

375g/13oz plaice or sole fillets, or thicker
    fish such as cod or haddock
a little flour
oil, for deep-frying
salt and ground black pepper
dill sprigs, to garnish

For the cream sauce

60ml/4 tbsp soured cream
60ml/4 tbsp mayonnaise
2.5ml/$\frac{1}{2}$ tsp grated lemon rind
30ml/2 tbsp chopped gherkins or capers
15ml/1 tbsp chopped mixed fresh herbs,
    or 5ml/1 tsp dried

For the batter

75g/3oz/$\frac{3}{4}$ cup plain flour
25g/1oz/$\frac{1}{4}$ cup grated Parmesan cheese
5ml/1 tsp bicarbonate of soda
1 egg, separated
150ml/$\frac{1}{4}$ pint/$\frac{2}{3}$ cup milk

1 To make the cream sauce, mix the soured cream, mayonnaise, lemon rind, gherkins or capers, herbs and seasoning together, then place in the fridge to chill.

2 To make the batter, sift the flour into a bowl. Mix in the other dry ingredients and some salt, and then whisk in the egg yolk and milk to give a thick yet smooth batter. Then gradually whisk in 90ml/6 tbsp water. Season and place in the fridge to chill.

3 Skin the fish and cut into thin strips of similar length. Season the flour and then dip the fish lightly in the flour.

4 Heat at least 5cm/2in oil in a large pan with a lid. Whisk the egg white until stiff and gently fold into the batter until just blended.

5 Dip the floured fish into the batter, drain off any excess and then drop gently into the hot fat.

6 Cook the fish in batches so that the goujons don't stick to one another for only 3–4 minutes, turning once. When the batter is golden and crisp, remove the fish with a slotted spoon. Place on kitchen paper on a plate and keep warm in a low oven while cooking the remaining goujons.

7 Serve hot garnished with sprigs of dill and accompanied by the cream sauce.

King Prawns in Crispy Batter

*Serve these delightfully crispy prawns
with an Oriental-style dipping
sauce, or offer a simple tomato sauce
or lemon wedges for squeezing.*

INGREDIENTS

Serves 4

120ml/4fl oz/¹⁄₂ cup water
1 egg
115g/4oz/1 cup plain flour
5ml/1 tsp cayenne pepper
12 raw king prawns, unpeeled
vegetable oil, for deep-frying
flat leaf parsley, to garnish
lemon wedges, to serve

For the dipping sauce
30ml/2 tbsp soy sauce
30ml/2 tbsp dry sherry
10ml/2 tsp clear honey

3 To make the dipping sauce, stir
together the soy sauce, dry
sherry and honey in a small bowl
until well combined.

4 Heat the oil in a large saucepan
or deep-fryer, until a cube of
stale bread tossed in browns in
1 minute.

5 Holding the prawns by their
tails, dip them into the batter,
one at a time, shaking off any
excess. Drop the prawns carefully
into the oil and fry for 2–3 minutes
until crisp and golden brown.
Drain on kitchen paper and serve
with the dipping sauce and lemon
wedges, garnished with parsley.

1 In a large bowl, whisk the water
with the egg. Add the flour and
cayenne, and whisk until smooth.

2 Carefully peel the prawns,
leaving just the tail sections
intact. Make a shallow cut down the
back of each prawn, then pull out
and discard the dark intestinal tract.

COOK'S TIP

Use leftover batter to coat thin
strips of sweet potato, beetroot,
carrot or pepper, then deep-fry
until golden.

Duck Wontons with Spicy Mango Sauce

These Chinese-style wontons are easy to make using ready-cooked smoked duck or chicken, or even leftovers from the Sunday roast.

INGREDIENTS

Makes about 40

15ml/1 tbsp light soy sauce

5ml/1 tsp sesame oil

2 spring onions, finely chopped

grated rind of ½ orange

5ml/1 tsp brown sugar

275g/10oz/1½ cups chopped
  smoked duck

about 40 small wonton wrappers

15ml/1 tbsp vegetable oil

whole fresh chives, to garnish (optional)

For the mango sauce

30ml/2 tbsp vegetable oil

5ml/1 tsp ground cumin

2.5ml/½ tsp ground cardamom

1.5ml/¼ tsp ground cinnamon

250ml/8fl oz/1 cup mango purée (about
  1 large mango)

15ml/1 tbsp clear honey

2.5ml/½ tsp Chinese chilli sauce (or
  to taste)

15ml/1 tbsp cider vinegar

snipped fresh chives, to garnish

2 Stir in the mango purée, honey, chilli sauce and vinegar. Remove from the heat and leave to cool. Pour into a bowl and cover until ready to serve.

3 Prepare the wonton filling. In a large bowl, mix together the soy sauce, sesame oil, spring onions, orange rind and brown sugar until well blended. Add the duck and toss to coat well.

1 First prepare the sauce. In a medium saucepan, heat the oil over a medium-low heat. Add the ground cumin, cardamom and cinnamon and cook for about 3 minutes, stirring constantly.

4 Place a teaspoonful of the duck mixture in the centre of each wonton wrapper. Brush the edges with water and then draw them up to the centre, twisting to seal and forming a pouch shape.

5 Preheat the oven to 190°F/ 375°C/Gas 5. Line a large baking sheet with foil and brush lightly with oil. Arrange the wontons on the baking sheet and bake for 10–12 minutes until crisp and golden. Serve with the mango sauce garnished with snipped fresh chives. If you wish, tie each wonton with a fresh chive.

COOK'S TIP

Wonton wrappers, available in some large supermarkets and Asian food shops, are sold in 450g/1lb packets and can be stored in the freezer almost indefinitely. Remove as many as you need, keeping the rest frozen.

Pork and Peanut Wontons with Plum Sauce

These crispy filled wontons are delicious served with a sweet plum sauce. The wontons can be filled and set aside for up to 8 hours before they are cooked.

INGREDIENTS

Makes 40–50 wontons

175g/6oz/1½ cups minced pork or
    175g/6oz pork sausages, skinned
2 spring onions, finely chopped
30ml/2 tbsp peanut butter
10ml/2 tsp oyster sauce (optional)
40–50 wonton skins
30ml/2 tbsp flour paste
vegetable oil, for deep-frying
salt and ground black pepper
lettuces and radishes, to garnish

For the plum sauce
225g/8oz/generous ¾ cup dark plum jam
15ml/1 tbsp rice or white wine vinegar
15ml/1 tbsp dark soy sauce
2.5ml/½ tsp chilli sauce

1 Combine the minced pork or skinned sausages, spring onions, peanut butter, oyster sauce, if using, and seasoning, and then set aside.

2 For the plum sauce, combine the plum jam, vinegar, soy and chilli sauces in a serving bowl and set aside.

3 To fill the wonton skins, place 8 wrappers at a time on a work surface, moisten the edges with the flour paste and place 2.5ml/½ tsp of the filling on each one. Fold in half, corner to corner, and twist.

4 Fill a wok or deep frying pan one-third with vegetable oil and heat to 190°C/385°F. Have ready a wire strainer or frying basket and a tray lined with kitchen paper. Drop the wontons, 8 at a time, into the hot fat and fry until golden all over, for about 1–2 minutes. Lift out on to the paper-lined tray and sprinkle with fine salt. Serve with the plum sauce garnished with lettuce and radishes.

Pork Balls with a Minted Peanut Sauce

This recipe is equally delicious made with chicken breasts.

INGREDIENTS

Serves 4–6

275g/10oz leg of pork, trimmed and diced

1cm/½in piece fresh root ginger, peeled and grated

1 garlic clove, crushed

10ml/2 tsp sesame oil

15ml/1 tbsp medium-dry sherry

15ml/1 tbsp soy sauce

5ml/1 tsp sugar

1 egg white

2.5ml/½ tsp salt

pinch of white pepper

350g/12oz/scant 1¾ cups long grain rice, washed and cooked for 15 minutes

50g/2oz ham, diced

1 iceberg or bib lettuce, to serve

For the peanut sauce

15ml/1 tbsp creamed coconut

75ml/2½fl oz/⅓ cup boiling water

30ml/2 tbsp smooth peanut butter

juice of 1 lime

1 red chilli, seeded and finely chopped

1 garlic clove, crushed

15ml/1 tbsp chopped fresh mint

15ml/1 tbsp chopped fresh coriander

15ml/1 tbsp fish sauce (optional)

1 Place the pork, ginger and garlic in a food processor; process for 2–3 minutes until smooth. Add the sesame oil, sherry, soy sauce and sugar and blend with the pork mixture. Finally, add the egg white, salt and white pepper.

2 Spread the cooked rice and ham in a shallow dish. Using wet hands, shape the pork mixture into thumb-size balls. Roll in the rice to coat and pierce each ball with a bamboo skewer.

3 To make the peanut sauce, put the creamed coconut in a measuring jug and cover with the boiling water. Place the peanut butter in another bowl with the lime juice, chilli, garlic, mint and coriander. Combine evenly then add the creamed coconut and season with the fish sauce if using.

4 Place the pork balls in a bamboo steamer then steam over a saucepan of boiling water for 8–10 minutes. Arrange the pork balls on lettuce leaves on a plate with the sauce to one side.

Chicken Satay with Peanut Sauce

These skewers of marinated chicken can be prepared in advance and served at room temperature. Beef, pork or even lamb fillet can be used instead of chicken if you prefer.

INGREDIENTS

Makes about 24

450g/1lb boneless, skinless chicken breasts

oil, for brushing

sesame seeds, for sprinkling

red pepper strips, to garnish

For the marinade

90ml/6 tbsp vegetable oil

60ml/4 tbsp tamari or light soy sauce

60ml/4 tbsp fresh lime juice

2.5cm/1in piece fresh root ginger, peeled
  and chopped

3–4 garlic cloves

30ml/2 tbsp light brown sugar

5ml/1 tsp Chinese-style chilli sauce or
  1 small red chilli pepper, seeded
  and chopped

30ml/2 tbsp chopped fresh coriander

For the peanut sauce

30ml/2 tbsp smooth peanut butter

30ml/2 tbsp soy sauce

15ml/1 tbsp sesame or vegetable oil

2 spring onions, chopped

2 garlic cloves

15–30ml/1–2 tbsp fresh lime or
  lemon juice

15ml/1 tbsp brown sugar

COOK'S TIP

When using metal skewers, look for flat ones which prevent the food from spinning around. If using wooden skewers, be sure to soak them in cold water for at least 30 minutes, to prevent them from burning.

1 Prepare the marinade. Place all the marinade ingredients in a food processor or blender and process until smooth and well blended, scraping down the sides of the bowl once. Pour into a shallow dish and set aside.

2 Into the same food processor or blender, put all the peanut sauce ingredients and process until well blended. If the sauce is too thick, add a little water and process again. Pour into a small bowl and cover until ready to serve.

3 Slice the chicken breasts into thin strips, then cut the strips into 2cm/ ¾ in pieces.

4 Add the chicken pieces to the marinade in the dish. Toss well to coat, cover and marinate for about 3–4 hours in a cool place, or overnight in the fridge.

5 Preheat the grill. Line a baking sheet with foil and brush lightly with oil. Thread 2–3 pieces of marinated chicken on to skewers and sprinkle with the sesame seeds. Grill for 4–5 minutes until golden, turning once. Serve with the peanut sauce, and a garnish of red pepper strips.

King Prawns with Spicy Dip

The spicy dip served with this dish is equally good made from peanuts instead of cashew nuts. Vegetarians can enjoy this, too, if you make it with vegetables or tofu cubes.

INGREDIENTS

Serves 4–6

24 raw king prawns, unpeeled

juice of ½ lemon

5ml/1 tsp paprika

1 bay leaf

1 thyme sprig

vegetable oil, for brushing

salt and ground black pepper

For the spicy dip

1 onion, chopped

4 canned plum tomatoes, plus 60ml/4 tbsp of the juice

½ green pepper, seeded and chopped

1 garlic clove, crushed

15ml/1 tbsp cashew nuts

15ml/1 tbsp soy sauce

15ml/1 tbsp desiccated coconut

3 To make the spicy dip, place all the ingredients in a blender or food processor and process until the mixture is smooth.

4 Pour into a saucepan with the prawn stock and simmer over a moderate heat for 30 minutes, until the sauce is fairly thick.

5 Preheat the grill. Thread the prawns on to small skewers, then brush the prawns on both sides with a little oil and grill under a low heat until cooked, turning once. Serve with the dip.

> ### COOK'S TIP
> ❧
>
> If unshelled raw prawns are not available, use cooked king prawns instead. Just grill them for a short time, until they are completely heated through.

1 Peel the prawns, leaving the tails on. Place in a shallow dish and sprinkle with the lemon juice, paprika and seasoning. Cover and chill in the fridge.

2 Put the shells in a saucepan with the bay leaf and thyme, cover with water, and bring to the boil. Simmer for 30 minutes; strain the stock into a measuring jug. Top up with some water, if necessary, to 300ml/½ pint/1¼ cups.

Beef Satay with a Hot Mango Dip

Strips of tender beef are flavoured with a delicious spicy marinade before being grilled then served with a fruit dip.

INGREDIENTS

Makes 12 skewers

450g/1lb sirloin steak,
   2cm/¾ in thick, trimmed

For the marinade

15ml/1 tbsp coriander seeds

5ml/1 tsp cumin seeds

50g/2oz/⅓ cup raw cashew nuts

15ml/1 tbsp vegetable oil

2 shallots, or 1 small onion, finely chopped

1cm/½in piece fresh root ginger, peeled
   and finely chopped

1 garlic clove, crushed

30ml/2 tbsp tamarind sauce

30ml/2 tbsp dark soy sauce

10ml/2 tsp sugar

5ml/1 tsp rice or white wine vinegar

For the mango dip

1 ripe mango

1–2 small red chillies, seeded and
   finely chopped

15ml/1 tbsp fish sauce

juice of 1 lime

10ml/2 tsp sugar

1.5ml/¼ tsp salt

30ml/2 tbsp chopped fresh coriander

1 Soak 12 bamboo skewers for 30 minutes. Slice the beef into long narrow strips and thread, zigzag-style, on to the skewers. Lay on a flat plate and set aside.

2 For the marinade, dry-fry the seeds and nuts in a large wok until evenly brown. Transfer to a mortar with a rough surface and crush finely with the pestle. Add the oil, shallots or onion, ginger, garlic, tamarind and soy sauces, sugar and rice or white wine vinegar.

3 Spread this marinade over the beef and leave to marinate for up to 8 hours. Cook the beef under a moderate grill or over a barbecue for 6–8 minutes, turning to ensure an even colour. Meanwhile, make the mango dip.

4 Cut away the skin and remove the stone from the mango. Process the mango flesh with the chillies, fish sauce, lime juice, sugar and salt until smooth, then add the coriander.

Skewered Lamb with Red Onion Salsa

This summery tapas dish is ideal for outdoor eating, although, if the weather fails, the skewers can be grilled rather than barbecued. The simple salsa makes a refreshing accompaniment – make sure that you use a mild-flavoured red onion that is fresh and crisp, and a tomato which is ripe and full of flavour.

INGREDIENTS

Serves 4

225g/8oz lean lamb, cubed

2.5ml/½ tsp ground cumin

5ml/1 tsp paprika

15ml/1 tbsp olive oil

salt and ground black pepper

For the salsa

1 red onion, very thinly sliced

1 large tomato, seeded and chopped

15ml/1 tbsp red wine vinegar

3–4 fresh basil or mint leaves,
    coarsely torn

small mint leaves, to garnish

1 Place the lamb in a bowl with the cumin, paprika, olive oil and plenty of salt and pepper. Toss well until the lamb is coated with spices.

2 Cover the bowl with clear film and set aside in a cool place for a few hours, or in the fridge overnight, so that the lamb absorbs the flavours.

3 Spear the lamb cubes on four small skewers – if using wooden skewers, soak first in cold water for 30 minutes to prevent them from burning.

4 To make the salsa, put the sliced onion, tomato, red wine vinegar and basil or mint leaves in a small bowl and stir together until thoroughly blended. Season to taste with salt, garnish with mint, then set aside while you cook the lamb skewers.

5 Cook over the barbecue or under a preheated grill for 5–10 minutes, turning frequently, until the lamb is well browned but still slightly pink in the centre. Serve hot, with the salsa.

Five-spice Rib-sticker

Choose the meatiest spare ribs you can, to make these a real success.

INGREDIENTS

Serves 8

1kg/2¼ lb pork spare ribs
10ml/2 tsp Chinese five-spice powder
2 garlic cloves, crushed
15ml/1 tbsp grated fresh root ginger
2.5ml/½ tsp chilli sauce
60ml/ 4 tbsp dark muscovado sugar
15ml/1 tbsp sunflower oil
4 spring onions

3 Cook the spare ribs under a preheated medium-hot grill turning frequently, for 30–40 minutes. Brush the ribs occasionally with the remaining marinade.

4 While the ribs are cooking, finely slice the spring onions – on the diagonal. To serve, place the ribs on a serving plate and scatter the spring onions over the top.

1 If the spare ribs are still attached together, cut between them to separate them (or ask your butcher to do this). Place the spare ribs in a large bowl.

2 Mix together all the remaining ingredients, except the spring onions, and pour over the ribs. Toss well to coat evenly. Cover the bowl and leave to marinate in the fridge overnight.

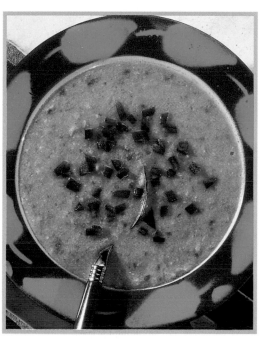

SOUPS

Cold Cucumber and Yogurt Soup

This refreshing cold soup uses the classic combination of cucumber and yogurt, with the added flavour of garlic and pleasant crunch of walnuts.

INGREDIENTS

Serves 5–6

1 cucumber

4 garlic cloves

2.5ml/½ tsp salt

75g/3oz/¾ cup walnut pieces

40g/1½ oz day-old bread, torn into pieces

30ml/2 tbsp walnut or sunflower oil

400ml/14fl oz/1⅔ cups sheep's or
    cow's yogurt

120ml/4fl oz/½ cup cold water or chilled
    still mineral water

5–10ml/1–2 tsp lemon juice

40g/1½oz/scant ½ cup walnuts, chopped,
    to garnish

olive oil, for drizzling

dill sprigs, to garnish

1 Cut the cucumber into two and peel one half of it. Dice the cucumber flesh and set aside.

2 Using a large pestle and mortar, crush the garlic and salt together well, then add the walnuts and bread.

3 When the mixture is smooth, add the walnut or sunflower oil slowly and combine well.

4 Transfer the walnut and bread mixture to a large bowl then beat in the cow's or sheep's yogurt and the diced cucumber.

5 Add the cold water or mineral water and lemon juice to taste.

6 Pour the soup into chilled soup bowls to serve. Garnish with the chopped walnuts, a little olive oil drizzled over the nuts and sprigs of dill.

COOK'S TIP

If you prefer your soup smooth, purée it in a food processor or blender before serving.

Chilled Tomato and Sweet Pepper Soup

This recipe was inspired by the Spanish gazpacho, the difference being that this soup is cooked first, and then chilled.

INGREDIENTS

Serves 4

2 red peppers, halved, cored and seeded

45ml/3 tbsp olive oil

1 onion, finely chopped

2 garlic cloves, crushed

675g/1½ lb ripe well-flavoured tomatoes

150ml/¼ pint/⅔ cup red wine

600ml/1 pint/2½ cups chicken stock

salt and ground black pepper

snipped fresh chives, to garnish

For the croûtons

2 slices white bread, crusts removed

60ml/4 tbsp olive oil

1 Cut each red pepper half into quarters. Place skin side up on a grill rack and cook until the skins are charred. Transfer to a bowl and cover with a plate or pop into a polythene bag and seal.

2 Heat the oil in a large pan. Add the onion and garlic and cook gently until soft. Meanwhile, remove the skin from the peppers and roughly chop the flesh. Cut the tomatoes into chunks.

3 Add the peppers and tomatoes to the pan, then cover and cook gently for 10 minutes. Add the wine and cook for a further 5 minutes, then add the stock and salt and pepper and continue to simmer for 20 minutes.

4 To make the croûtons, cut the bread into cubes. Heat the oil in a small frying pan, add the bread and fry until golden. Drain on kitchen paper and store in an airtight box.

5 Process the soup in a blender or food processor until smooth. Pour into a clean glass or ceramic bowl and leave to cool thoroughly before chilling in the fridge for at least 3 hours. When the soup is cold, season to taste.

6 Serve the soup in bowls, topped with the croûtons and garnished with snipped chives.

Chilled Asparagus Soup

This soup provides a delightful way to enjoy a favourite seasonal vegetable. Choose bright, crisp-looking asparagus with firm, slender stalks.

INGREDIENTS

Serves 6

900g/2lb fresh asparagus

60ml/4 tbsp butter or olive oil

175g/6oz/1½ cups sliced leeks or
    spring onions

45ml/3 tbsp flour

1.5 litres/2½ pints/6¼ cups chicken stock
    or water

120ml/4fl oz/½ cup single cream or
    plain yogurt

salt and ground black pepper

15ml/1 tbsp minced fresh tarragon or chervil

3 Heat the butter or olive oil in a heavy saucepan. Add the leeks or spring onions and cook over a low heat until softened, about 5–8 minutes. Stir in the chopped asparagus stalks, cover and cook for a further 6–8 minutes.

4 Add the flour and stir well to blend. Cook for 3–4 minutes, uncovered, stirring occasionally.

5 Add the stock or water and bring to the boil, stirring frequently, then reduce the heat and simmer for 30 minutes. Season with salt and pepper.

6 Purée the soup in a food processor or blender. If necessary, strain it to remove any coarse fibres. Stir in the asparagus tips, most of the cream or yogurt, and the herbs. Cool then chill well. Stir thoroughly before serving, and check the seasoning. Garnish with the remaining cream or yogurt.

1 Cut the top 6cm/2½in off the asparagus spears. Blanch these tips in boiling water until they are just tender, 5–6 minutes. Drain. Cut each tip into 2 or 3 pieces, and set aside.

2 Trim the ends of the stalks, removing any brown or woody parts. Chop the asparagus stalks into 1cm/½in pieces.

COOK'S TIP

Chilled soups can require extra seasoning, so remember to check the taste just before you serve.

Gazpacho with Avocado Salsa

Tomatoes, cucumber and peppers form the basis of this classic, chilled soup. Add a spoonful of chunky, fresh avocado salsa and a scattering of croûtons for a delicious summer starter. This is quite a substantial soup, so follow with a light main course, such as grilled fish or chicken.

INGREDIENTS

Serves 4–6

2 slices day-old bread
600ml/1 pint/2½ cups chilled water
1kg/2¼ lb tomatoes
1 cucumber
1 red pepper, seeded and chopped
1 green chilli, seeded and chopped
2 garlic cloves, chopped
30ml/2 tbsp extra virgin olive oil
juice of 1 lime and 1 lemon
few drops of Tabasco sauce
salt and ground black pepper
handful of fresh basil, to garnish
8–12 ice cubes, to serve

For the croûtons

2–3 slices day-old bread, crusts removed
1 garlic clove, halved
15–30ml/1–2 tbsp olive oil

For the avocado salsa

1 ripe avocado
5ml/1 tsp lemon juice
2.5cm/1in piece cucumber, diced
½ red chilli, finely chopped

1 Make the soup first. In a shallow bowl, soak the day-old bread in 150ml/¼ pint/⅔ cup water for 5 minutes.

COOK'S TIP

For a superior flavour choose Haas avocados with the rough-textured, almost black skins.

2 Meanwhile, place the tomatoes in a heatproof bowl; cover with boiling water. Leave for 30 seconds, then peel, seed and chop the flesh.

3 Thinly peel the cucumber, cut in half lengthways and scoop out the seeds with a teaspoon. Discard the seeds and chop the flesh.

4 Place the bread, tomatoes, cucumber, red pepper, chilli, garlic, oil, citrus juices, Tabasco and 450ml/¾ pint/scant 2 cups chilled water in a food processor or blender. Blend until mixed but still chunky. Season and chill well.

5 To make the croûtons, rub the slices of bread with the cut surface of the garlic clove. Cut the bread into cubes and place in a polythene bag with the olive oil. Seal the bag and shake until the bread cubes are coated with the oil. Heat a large non-stick frying pan and fry the croûtons over a medium heat until crisp and golden.

6 Just before serving make the avocado salsa. Halve the avocado, remove the stone, then peel and dice the flesh. Toss the avocado in the lemon juice to prevent it browning, then mix with the cucumber and chilli.

7 Ladle the soup into bowls, add the ice cubes, and top with a spoonful of avocado salsa. Garnish with the basil and hand round the croûtons separately.

Chilled Prawn and Cucumber Soup

*If you've never served a chilled soup
before, this is the one to try first.
Delicious and light, it's the perfect
way to celebrate summer.*

INGREDIENTS

Serves 4

25g/1oz/2 tbsp butter

2 shallots, finely chopped

2 garlic cloves, crushed

1 cucumber, peeled, seeded and diced

300ml/½ pint/1¼ cups milk

225g/8oz cooked peeled prawns

15ml/1 tbsp each finely chopped fresh
    mint, dill, chives and chervil

300ml/½ pint/1¼ cups whipping cream

salt and ground white pepper

For the garnish

30ml/2 tbsp crème fraîche or soured
    cream (optional)

4 large, cooked prawns, peeled with tail
    intact

fresh chives and dill

1 Melt the butter in a saucepan
and cook the shallots and
garlic over a low heat until soft but
not coloured. Add the cucumber
and cook the vegetables gently,
stirring frequently, until tender.

2 Stir in the milk, bring almost
to the boil, then lower the heat
and simmer for 5 minutes. Tip the
soup into a blender or food
processor and purée until very
smooth. Season to taste with salt
and ground white pepper.

3 Pour the soup into a bowl and
set aside to cool. When cool,
stir in the prawns, chopped herbs
and the whipping cream. Cover,
transfer to the fridge and chill for
at least 2 hours.

4 To serve, ladle the soup into
four individual bowls and top
each portion with a dollop of
crème fraîche or soured cream, if
using. Place a prawn over the edge
of each dish. Garnish with the
chives and dill.

COOK'S TIP

For a change try fresh or canned
crabmeat, or cooked, flaked
salmon fillet.

Hot-and-sour Soup

This light and invigorating soup originates from Thailand. It is traditionally served at the beginning of a formal Thai meal to stimulate the appetite.

INGREDIENTS

Serves 4

2 carrots

900ml/1½ pints/3¾ cups vegetable stock

2 Thai chillies, seeded and finely sliced

2 lemon grass stalks, outer leaves removed and each stalk cut into 3 pieces

4 kaffir lime leaves

2 garlic cloves, finely chopped

4 spring onions, finely sliced

5ml/1 tsp sugar

juice of 1 lime

45ml/3 tbsp chopped fresh coriander

salt, to taste

130g/4½ oz/1 cup Japanese tofu, sliced

1 To make carrot flowers, cut each carrot in half crossways, then, using a sharp knife, cut four V-shaped channels lengthways. Slice the carrots into thin rounds and set aside.

COOK'S TIP

Kaffir lime leaves have a distinctive citrus flavour. The fresh leaves can be bought from Asian shops, and some supermarkets now sell them dried.

2 Pour the vegetable stock into a large saucepan. Reserve 2.5ml/ ½ tsp of the chillies and add the rest to the pan with the lemon grass, lime leaves, garlic and half the spring onions. Bring to the boil, then reduce the heat and simmer for 20 minutes. Strain the stock and discard the flavourings.

3 Return the stock to the pan, add the reserved chillies and spring onions, the sugar, lime juice, coriander and salt to taste.

4 Simmer for 5 minutes, then add the carrot flowers and tofu slices, and cook the soup for a further 2 minutes until the carrot is just tender. Serve hot.

Sweetcorn Soup

This is a simple to make yet very flavoursome soup. It is sometimes made with soured cream and cream cheese. Poblano chillies may be added, but these are rather difficult to locate outside Mexico. However, you may be able to find them canned in some of the larger supermarkets and delicatessens.

INGREDIENTS

Serves 4

30ml/2 tbsp corn oil

1 onion, finely chopped

1 red pepper, seeded and chopped

450g/1lb sweetcorn kernels, thawed
   if frozen

750ml/1¼ pints/3 cups chicken stock

250ml/8fl oz/1 cup single cream

salt and ground black pepper

½ red pepper, seeded and finely diced,
   to garnish

1 Heat the oil in a frying pan and sauté the onion and red pepper for about 5 minutes, until soft. Add the sweetcorn and sauté for 2 minutes.

2 Carefully tip the contents of the pan into a food processor or blender. Process until the mixture is smooth, scraping down the sides and adding a little of the stock, if necessary.

3 Put the mixture into a clean saucepan and stir in the stock. Season to taste with salt and pepper, bring to a simmer and cook for 5 minutes.

4 Gently stir in the cream. Serve the soup hot or chilled, with the diced red pepper sprinkled over. If serving hot, reheat gently after adding the cream, but do not allow the soup to boil.

Courgette Soup

This soup is so simple – in terms of ingredients and preparation. It would provide an elegant start to a dinner party.

INGREDIENTS

Serves 4

30ml/2 tbsp butter

1 onion, finely chopped

450g/1lb young courgettes, trimmed
   and chopped

750ml/1¼ pints/3 cups chicken stock

120ml/4fl oz/½ cup single cream, plus
   extra to serve

salt and ground black pepper

1 Melt the butter in a saucepan and sauté the onion until it is soft. Add the courgettes and cook, stirring, for about 1–2 minutes.

2 Add the chicken stock. Bring to the boil over a moderate heat and then simmer for about 5 minutes or until the courgettes are just tender.

3 Strain the stock into a clean saucepan, saving the vegetable solids in the sieve. Purée the solids in the food processor and add to the pan. Season to taste with salt and pepper.

4 Stir the cream into the soup and heat through very gently without allowing it to the boil. Serve hot with a little extra cream swirled in.

> ### COOK'S TIP
> ∽
> Always use the smallest courgettes available, as these have the best flavour.

Pear and Watercress Soup

The pears in the soup are complemented beautifully by Stilton croûtons. Their flavours make them natural partners.

Serves 6

1 bunch watercress

4 pears, sliced

900ml/1½ pints/3¾ cups chicken stock, preferably home-made

120ml/4fl oz/½ cup double cream

juice of 1 lime

salt and ground black pepper

For the croûtons

25g/1oz/2 tbsp butter

15ml/1 tbsp olive oil

200g/7oz/3 cups cubed stale bread

150g/5oz/1 cup chopped Stilton

1 Keep back about a third of the watercress leaves. Place the rest of the leaves and stalks in a pan with the pears, stock and a little seasoning. Simmer for about 15–20 minutes. Reserving some watercress leaves for garnishing, add the rest of the leaves and then purée in a blender or food processor until smooth.

2 Put the mixture into a bowl and stir in the cream and the lime juice to mix the flavours thoroughly. Season again to taste. Pour all the soup back into a pan and reheat, stirring gently until warmed through.

3 To make the croûtons, melt the butter and oil and fry the bread cubes until golden brown. Drain on kitchen paper. Put the cheese on top and heat under a hot grill until bubbling. Reheat the soup and pour into bowls. Divide the croûtons and the reserved watercress leaves between the bowls and serve immediately.

Baby Carrot and Fennel Soup

Sweet tender carrots find their moment of glory in this delicately spiced soup. Fennel provides a very subtle aniseed flavour which does not overpower the carrots.

INGREDIENTS

Serves 4

50g/2oz/4 tbsp butter

1 small bunch spring onions, chopped

150g/5oz fennel bulb, chopped

1 celery stick, chopped

450g/1lb new carrots, grated

2.5ml/½ tsp ground cumin

150g/5oz new potatoes, peeled and diced

1.2 litres/2 pints/5 cups chicken or
   vegetable stock

60ml/4 tbsp double cream

salt and ground black pepper

60ml/4 tbsp chopped fresh parsley,
   to garnish

1 Melt the butter in a large saucepan and add the spring onions, fennel, celery, carrots and cumin. Cover and cook for about 5 minutes, or until soft.

2 Add the diced potatoes and chicken or vegetable stock, and simmer the mixture for a further 10 minutes.

3 Liquidize the soup in the pan with a hand-held blender. Stir in the cream and season to taste. Serve in individual soup bowls and garnish with chopped parsley.

COOK'S TIP

For convenience, you can freeze the soup in portions before adding the cream, seasoning and parsley.

Spanish Garlic Soup

This is a simple and satisfying soup, made with one of the most popular ingredients in the Mediterranean region – garlic!

INGREDIENTS

Serves 4

30ml/2 tbsp olive oil

4 large garlic cloves, peeled

4 slices French bread, 5mm/¼ in thick

15ml/1 tbsp paprika

1 litre/1¾ pints/4 cups beef stock

1.5ml/¼ tsp ground cumin

pinch of saffron strands

4 eggs

salt and ground black pepper

chopped fresh parsley, to garnish

1 Preheat the oven to 230°C/450°F/Gas 8. Heat the oil in a large pan. Add the whole garlic cloves and cook until golden. Remove and set aside. Fry the bread in the oil until golden, then set aside.

COOK'S TIP

Use home-made beef stock for the best flavour or buy prepared stock from your supermarket – you'll find it in the chilled counter. Never use stock cubes as they contain too much salt.

2 Add the paprika to the pan, and fry for a few seconds, stirring. Stir in the beef stock, the cumin and saffron, then add the reserved fried garlic, crushing the cloves with the back of a wooden spoon. Season with salt and ground black pepper then cook for about 5 minutes.

3 Ladle the soup into four ovenproof bowls and gently break an egg into each one. Place the slices of fried French bread on top of the eggs and place in the oven for about 3–4 minutes, or until the eggs are set. Sprinkle with chopped fresh parsley and serve at once.

Fresh Tomato Soup

Intensely flavoured sun-ripened tomatoes need little embellishment in this fresh-tasting soup. If you buy from the supermarket, choose the juiciest looking ones and add the amount of sugar and vinegar necessary, depending on their natural sweetness. On a hot day this Italian soup is also delicious chilled.

INGREDIENTS

Serves 6

1.3–1.6kg/3–3½ lb ripe tomatoes

400ml/14fl oz/1⅔ cups chicken or
   vegetable stock

45ml/3 tbsp sun dried tomato paste

30–45ml/2–3 tbsp balsamic vinegar

10–15ml/2–3 tsp caster sugar

small handful of basil leaves

salt and ground black pepper

basil leaves, to garnish

toasted cheese croûtes and crème fraîche,
   to serve

1 Plunge the tomatoes into boiling water for 30 seconds, then refresh in cold water. Peel away the skins and quarter the tomatoes. Put them in a large saucepan and pour over the chicken or vegetable stock. Bring just to the boil, reduce the heat, cover and simmer the mixture gently for 10 minutes until the tomatoes are pulpy.

2 Stir in the tomato paste, vinegar, sugar and basil. Season with salt and pepper, then cook gently, stirring, for 2 minutes. Process the soup in a blender or food processor, then return to the pan and reheat gently. Serve in bowls topped with one or two toasted cheese croûtes and a spoonful of crème fraîche, garnished with basil leaves.

Avocado Soup

To add a subtle garlic flavour, rub the cut side of a garlic clove around the soup bowls before adding the soup.

INGREDIENTS

Serves 4

2 large ripe avocados

1 litre/1¾ pints/4 cups chicken stock

250ml/8fl oz/1 cup single cream

salt and ground white pepper

15ml/1 tbsp finely chopped coriander, to garnish (optional)

2 Heat the chicken stock with the cream in a saucepan. When the mixture is hot, but not boiling, whisk it into the puréed avocado.

3 Season to taste with salt and pepper. Serve immediately, sprinkled with the coriander, if using. The soup may be served chilled, if liked.

1 Cut the avocados in half, remove the stones and mash the flesh (see Cook's Tip). Put the flesh into a sieve and with a wooden spoon, press it through into a warmed bowl.

COOK'S TIP

The easiest way to mash the avocados is to hold each seeded half in turn in the palm of one hand and mash the flesh in the shell with a fork, before scooping it into the bowl. This avoids the avocado slithering about when it is being mashed.

Vermicelli Soup

The inclusion of fresh coriander adds a piquancy to this soup and complements the tomato flavour.

INGREDIENTS

Serves 4

30ml/2 tbsp olive or corn oil

50g/2oz vermicelli

1 onion, roughly chopped

1 garlic clove, chopped

450g/1lb tomatoes, peeled, seeded and
  roughly chopped

1 litre/1¾ pints/4 cups chicken stock

1.5ml/¼ tsp sugar

15ml/1 tbsp finely chopped fresh
  coriander

salt and ground black pepper

chopped fresh coriander, to garnish

25g/1oz/¼ cup freshly grated Parmesan
  cheese, to serve

1 Heat the oil in a frying pan and sauté the vermicelli over a moderate heat until golden brown. Take care not to let the strands burn. Remove the vermicelli with a slotted spoon or tongs and drain on kitchen paper.

2 Purée the onion, garlic and tomatoes in a food processor or blender until smooth. Return the frying pan to the heat. When the oil is hot again, add the purée to the pan. Cook, stirring constantly to prevent sticking, for about 5 minutes or until thick.

3 Transfer the purée to a saucepan. Add the vermicelli and pour in the stock. Season with sugar, salt and pepper. Stir in the coriander, bring to the boil, then lower the heat, cover the pan and simmer the soup gently until the vermicelli is tender.

4 Serve in warmed soup bowls, sprinkle with chopped fresh coriander and offer the grated Parmesan cheese separately.

COOK'S TIP

Vermicelli burns very easily, so move it about continuously in the frying pan with a wooden spoon and remove it from the heat as soon as it turns a golden brown colour.

Wild Mushroom Soup

Wild mushrooms are expensive, but dried porcini have an intense flavour, so only a small quantity is needed. The beef stock may seem unusual in a vegetable soup, but it helps to strengthen the earthy flavour of the mushrooms.

INGREDIENTS

Serves 4

25g/1oz/1 cup dried porcini mushrooms

30ml/2 tbsp olive oil

15g/½ oz/1 tbsp butter

2 leeks, thinly sliced

2 shallots, roughly chopped

1 garlic clove, roughly chopped

225g/8oz/3 cups fresh wild mushrooms

about 1.2 litres/2 pints/5 cups beef stock

2.5ml/½ tsp dried thyme

150ml/¼ pint/⅔ cup double cream

salt and ground black pepper

thyme sprigs, to garnish

1 Put the dried porcini in a bowl, add 250ml/8fl oz/1 cup warm water and leave to soak for 20–30 minutes. Lift out of the liquid and squeeze over the bowl to remove as much of the soaking liquid as possible. Strain all the liquid and reserve to use later. Finely chop the porcini.

2 Heat the oil and butter in a large saucepan until foaming. Add the sliced leeks, chopped shallots and garlic and cook gently for about 5 minutes, stirring frequently, until soft.

3 Chop or slice the fresh wild mushrooms and add to the pan. Stir over a medium heat for a few minutes until they begin to soften. Pour in the stock and bring to the boil. Add the porcini, their soaking liquid, the dried thyme and salt and ground black pepper. Lower the heat, half cover the pan and simmer the soup gently for 30 minutes, stirring occasionally.

4 Pour about three-quarters of the soup into a blender or food processor and process until very smooth. Return the purée to the soup remaining in the pan, stir in the cream and heat through. Check the consistency and add a little more stock or water if the soup is too thick. Taste for seasoning. Serve hot garnished with thyme sprigs.

Spinach and Bean Curd Soup

This soup is really delicious. If fresh spinach is not in season, watercress or lettuce can be used instead.

INGREDIENTS

Serves 4

1 cake bean curd, 7.5cm/3in sq. and
   2.5cm/1in thick
115g/4oz spinach leaves
750ml/1¼ pints/3 cups vegetable stock
15ml/1 tbsp light soy sauce
salt and ground black pepper

1 Rinse the bean curd then cut into 12 small pieces, each about 5mm/¼in thick. Wash the spinach leaves and cut them into small pieces.

2 In a wok or saucepan, bring the stock to a rolling boil. Add the bean curd and soy sauce, bring back to the boil and simmer for about 2 minutes.

3 Add the spinach and simmer for a further minute. Skim the surface to make it clear, then add salt and ground black pepper to taste, and serve.

Salmon Chowder

A variation on the classic prawn chowder, this salmon version is equally delicious.

Serves 4–6

20g/³⁄₄oz/1¹⁄₂ tbsp butter or margarine

1 onion, minced

1 leek, minced

50g/2oz/¹⁄₂ cup minced bulb fennel

25g/1oz/¹⁄₄ cup plain flour

1.5 litres/2¹⁄₂ pints 6¹⁄₄ cups fish stock

225g/8oz potatoes, cut into 1cm/¹⁄₂in cubes (about 2 medium-size potatoes)

salt and ground black pepper

450g/1lb boneless, skinless salmon, cut into 2cm/³⁄₄in cubes

175ml/6fl oz/³⁄₄ cup milk

120ml/4fl oz/¹⁄₂ cup whipping cream

30ml/2 tbsp chopped fresh dill

4 Add the cubed salmon and then simmer until just cooked, about 3–5 minutes. The cubes should remain intact, not fall apart.

5 Stir in the milk, cream and dill. Cook until just warmed through; do not boil. Taste and adjust the seasoning if necessary, then serve.

1 Melt the butter or margarine in a large saucepan. Add the onion, leek and fennel and cook over a medium heat until the vegetables are softened, about 5–8 minutes, stirring occasionally.

2 Stir in the flour. Reduce the heat to low and cook, stirring occasionally to prevent any lumps forming, for 3 minutes.

3 Add the stock and potatoes. Season with salt and ground black pepper. Bring to the boil, then reduce the heat, cover and simmer until the potatoes are tender, about 20 minutes.

Tomato and Blue Cheese Soup with Bacon

As blue cheese is rather salty, it is important to use unsalted stock for this flavoursome soup.

INGREDIENTS

Serves 4

1.3kg/3lb ripe tomatoes, peeled, quartered
    and seeded
2 garlic cloves, crushed
30ml/2 tbsp vegetable oil or butter
1 leek, chopped
1 carrot, chopped
1 litre/1¾ pints/4 cups unsalted
    chicken stock
115g/4oz Danish blue cheese, crumbled
45ml/3 tbsp whipping cream
several large fresh basil leaves, or 1–2 fresh
    parsley sprigs
salt and ground black pepper
175g/6oz bacon, cooked and crumbled,
    to garnish

1 Preheat the oven to 200°C/400°F/Gas 6. Spread the tomatoes in a baking dish. Sprinkle with the garlic and some salt and ground black pepper. Place in the oven and bake for 35 minutes.

2 Heat the oil or butter in a large saucepan. Add the leek and carrot and season lightly with salt and pepper. Cook over a low heat, stirring often, for 10 minutes or until softened.

3 Stir in the chicken stock and baked tomatoes. Bring to the boil, lower the heat, cover and simmer for 20 minutes.

4 Add the blue cheese, cream, and basil or parsley. Transfer to a food processor or blender and process until smooth (working in batches if necessary). Taste for seasoning; adjust if needed.

5 If necessary, reheat the soup, but do not let it boil. Ladle into warmed bowls and scatter the crumbled bacon over.

Tortellini Chanterelle Broth

The savoury-sweet quality of chanterelle mushrooms combines well in a simple broth with spinach-and-ricotta-filled tortellini. The addition of a little sherry creates a lovely warming effect.

INGREDIENTS

Serves 4

350g/12oz fresh spinach and ricotta
tortellini, or 175g/6oz dried

1.2 litres/2 pints/5 cups chicken stock

75ml/5 tbsp dry sherry

175g/6oz fresh chanterelle mushrooms,
trimmed and sliced, or 15g/½ oz/½ cup
dried chanterelles

chopped fresh parsley, to garnish

1 Cook the tortellini according to the packet instructions.

2 Bring the chicken stock to the boil, add the dry sherry and fresh or dried mushrooms and simmer for 10 minutes.

3 Strain the tortellini, add to the stock, then ladle the broth into four warmed soup bowls, making sure each contains the same proportions of tortellini and mushrooms. Garnish with the chopped parsley and serve.

French Onion and Morel Soup

French onion soup is appreciated for its light beefy taste. There are few improvements to be made to this classic soup, but a few richly scented morel mushrooms will impart a worthwhile flavour.

Serves 4

50g/2oz/4 tbsp unsalted butter, plus extra
    for spreading
15ml/1 tbsp vegetable oil
3 onions, sliced
900ml/1½ pints/3¾ cups beef stock
75ml/5 tbsp Madeira or sherry
8 dried morel mushrooms
4 slices French bread
75g/3oz Gruyère, Beaufort or Fontina
    cheese, grated
30ml/2 tbsp chopped fresh parsley

1 Melt the butter with the oil in a large frying pan, then add the sliced onions and cook gently for 10–15 minutes until the onions are a rich mahogany brown colour.

2 Transfer the browned onions to a large saucepan, cover with beef stock, add the Madeira or sherry and the dried morels, then simmer for 20 minutes.

COOK'S TIP

The flavour and richness of this soup will improve with keeping. Chill for up to 5 days.

3 Preheat the grill to a moderate temperature and toast the French bread on both sides. Spread one side with butter and heap with the grated cheese. Ladle the soup into four flameproof bowls, float the cheesy toasts on top and grill until they are crisp and brown. Alternatively, grill the cheese-topped toast, then place one slice in each warmed soup bowl before ladling the hot soup over it. The toast will float to the surface. Scatter over the chopped fresh parsley and serve.

Curried Parsnip Soup

The spices impart a delicious, mild curry flavour which carries an exotic breath of India.

Serves 4

30ml/2 tbsp butter

1 garlic clove, crushed

1 onion, chopped

5ml/1 tsp ground cumin

5ml/1 tsp ground coriander

4 parsnips, peeled and sliced

10ml/2 tsp medium curry paste

450ml/¾ pint/scant 2 cups chicken stock

450ml/¾ pint/scant 2 cups milk

60ml/4 tbsp soured cream

squeeze of lemon juice

salt and ground black pepper

fresh chives, to garnish

ready-made garlic and coriander naan bread, to serve

1 Heat the butter in a large pan and add the garlic and onion. Fry gently for 4–5 minutes, until lightly golden. Stir in the cumin and coriander and cook for a further 1–2 minutes.

2 Add the parsnips and stir until well coated with the butter, then stir in the curry paste, followed by the stock. Cover the pan and simmer for 15 minutes, until the parsnips are tender.

3 Ladle the soup into a blender or food processor and then process until smooth.

4 Return the soup to the pan and stir in the milk. Heat gently for 2–3 minutes, then add half the soured cream and all the lemon juice. Season well.

5 Serve in bowls topped with swirls of the remaining soured cream and the chopped fresh chives, accompanied by the naan bread.

Malayan Prawn Laksa

This spicy prawn and noodle soup tastes just as good when made with fresh crab meat or any flaked cooked fish. If you are short of time or can't find all the spicy paste ingredients, buy ready-made laksa paste, which is available from Oriental stores.

INGREDIENTS

Serves 3–4

115g/4oz rice vermicelli or stir-fry
   rice noodles
15ml/1 tbsp vegetable or groundnut oil
600ml/1 pint/2½ cups fish stock
400ml/14fl oz/1⅔ cups thin coconut milk
30ml/2 tbsp *nam pla* (Thai fish sauce)
½ lime
16–24 cooked peeled prawns
salt and cayenne pepper
60ml/4 tbsp fresh coriander sprigs and
   leaves, chopped, to garnish

For the spicy paste
2 lemon grass stalks, finely chopped
2 fresh red chillies, seeded and chopped
2.5cm/1in piece fresh root ginger, peeled
   and sliced
2.5ml/½ tsp *blachan* (dried shrimp paste)
2 garlic cloves, chopped
2.5ml/½ tsp ground turmeric
30ml/2 tbsp tamarind paste

1 Cook the rice vermicelli or noodles in a large saucepan of boiling salted water according to the instructions on the packet. Tip into a large sieve or colander, then rinse under cold water and drain. Set aside and keep warm.

2 To make the spicy paste, place all the ingredients in a mortar and pound with a pestle. Or, if you prefer, put the ingredients in a food processor or blender and then process until a smooth paste is formed.

3 Heat the oil in a large saucepan, add the spicy paste and fry, stirring constantly, for a few moments to release all the flavours, but be careful not to let it burn.

4 Add the fish stock and coconut milk and bring to the boil. Stir in the *nam pla*, then simmer for 5 minutes. Season with salt and cayenne to taste, adding a squeeze of lime. Add the prawns and heat through for a few seconds.

5 Divide the noodles among three or four soup plates. Pour the soup over, making sure that each portion includes an equal number of prawns. Garnish with coriander and serve piping hot.

Broccoli Soup with Garlic Toast

This is an Italian recipe, originating from Rome. For the best flavour and colour, use the freshest broccoli you can find.

INGREDIENTS

Serves 6

675g/1½ lb broccoli spears
1.75 litres/3 pints/7½ cups chicken or
    vegetable stock
salt and ground black pepper
30ml/2 tbsp fresh lemon juice
freshly grated Parmesan cheese
    (optional), to serve

For the garlic toast
6 slices white bread
1 large clove garlic, halved

1 Using a small sharp knife, peel the broccoli stems, starting from the base of the stalks and pulling gently up towards the florets. (The peel comes off very easily.) Chop the broccoli into small chunks.

2 Bring the stock to the boil in a large saucepan. Add the chopped broccoli and simmer for 30 minutes, or until soft.

COOK'S TIP

As this is an Italian recipe, choose a really good quality Parmesan cheese, if you are using it. The very best is Italy's own Parmigiano-Reggiano.

3 Purée about half of the soup in a blender or food processor and then mix into the rest of the soup. Season with salt, pepper and lemon juice.

4 Just before serving, reheat the soup to just below boiling point. Toast the bread, rub with garlic and cut into quarters. Place 3 or 4 pieces of toast in the base of each soup plate. Ladle on the soup. Serve at once, with grated Parmesan cheese if wished.

Spinach and Rice Soup

Use very fresh, young spinach leaves in the preparation of this light and fresh-tasting soup.

INGREDIENTS

Serves 4

675g/1½ lb fresh spinach, washed

45ml/3 tbsp extra virgin olive oil

1 small onion, finely chopped

2 garlic cloves, finely chopped

1 small fresh red chilli, seeded and finely chopped

115g/4oz/generous 1 cup risotto rice

1.2 litres/2 pints/5 cups vegetable stock

salt and ground black pepper

60ml/4 tbsp grated Pecorino cheese

1 Place the spinach in a large pan with just the water that clings to its leaves after washing. Add a large pinch of salt. Heat gently until the spinach has wilted, then remove from the heat and drain, reserving any liquid.

2 Either chop the spinach finely using a large knife or place in a food processor and process to a fairly coarse purée.

COOK'S TIP

Pecorino, made from sheep's milk, has a slightly sharper taste than its cow's milk counterpart, Parmesan. However, if you cannot find it, use Parmesan instead.

3 Heat the oil in a large saucepan and gently cook the onion, garlic and chilli for 4–5 minutes until softened. Stir in the rice until well coated, then pour in the stock and reserved spinach liquid. Bring to the boil, lower the heat and simmer for 10 minutes. Add the spinach, with salt and ground black pepper to taste. Cook for a further 5–7 minutes, until the rice is tender. Check the seasoning and adjust if needed. Serve with the Pecorino cheese.

Split Pea Soup

This tasty winter soup is a perfect family starter, and can be made using left over cold ham if necessary.

Serves 4–6

25g/1oz/2 tbsp butter

1 large onion, chopped

1 large celery stalk with leaves, chopped

2 carrots, chopped

1 smoked gammon knuckle, 450g/1lb

2 litres/3½ pints/8½ cups water

350g/12oz/1½ cups split peas

30ml/2 tbsp chopped fresh parsley, plus extra to garnish

2.5ml/½ tsp dried thyme

1 bay leaf

about 30ml/2 tbsp lemon juice

salt and ground black pepper

3 After 2 hours, once the peas are very tender, remove the gammon knuckle. Leave it to cool a bit, then remove the skin and cut the meat from the bones. Discard the skin and bones, then cut the meat into chunks as evenly sized as possible.

4 Return the chunks of gammon to the soup. Discard the bay leaf. Taste and adjust the seasoning with more lemon juice, salt and pepper.

5 Serve hot, sprinkled with fresh parsley.

1 Melt the butter in a large heavy-based saucepan. Add the onion, celery and carrots and cook until soft, stirring occasionally.

2 Place all the rest of the ingredients in the pan. Bring to the boil, cover and simmer gently for 2 hours.

Fish Soup with Rouille

Making this soup is simplicity itself, yet the flavour suggests it is the product of painstaking preparation and complicated cooking.

INGREDIENTS

Serves 6

1kg/2¼ lb mixed fish

30ml/2 tbsp olive oil

1 onion, chopped

1 carrot, chopped

1 leek, chopped

2 large ripe tomatoes, chopped

1 red pepper, seeded and chopped

2 garlic cloves, peeled

150g/5oz/⅔ cup tomato purée

1 large fresh bouquet garni, containing 3
    parsley sprigs, 3 small celery sticks and
    3 bay leaves

300ml/½ pint/1¼ cups dry white wine

salt and ground black pepper

For the rouille

2 garlic cloves, roughly chopped

5ml/1 tsp coarse salt

1 thick slice of white bread, crust
    removed, soaked in water and then
    squeezed dry

1 fresh red chilli, seeded and roughly
    chopped

45ml/3 tbsp olive oil

salt, to taste

pinch of cayenne pepper (optional)

For the garnish

12 slices of baguette, toasted in the oven

50g/2oz Gruyère cheese, finely grated

1 Cut the fish into 7.5cm/3in chunks, removing any obvious bones. Heat the olive oil in a large saucepan, then add the prepared fish and chopped vegetables. Stir gently until the vegetables begin to colour.

2 Now add all the other soup ingredients, then pour in just enough cold water to cover the mixture. Season well and bring to just below boiling point, then lower the heat so that the soup is barely simmering, cover and cook for 1 hour.

3 Meanwhile, make the rouille. Put the garlic and coarse salt in a mortar and crush to a paste with a pestle. Add the soaked bread and chilli and pound until smooth, or purée in a food processor. Whisk in the olive oil, a drop at a time, to make a smooth, shiny sauce that resembles mayonnaise. Season with salt and add a pinch of cayenne if you like. Set aside.

4 Lift out and discard the bouquet garni. Purée the soup in batches in a food processor, then strain through a fine sieve into a clean pan, pushing the solids through with a ladle.

5 Reheat the soup but do not boil. Check the seasoning and ladle into individual bowls. Top each with two slices of toasted baguette, a spoonful of rouille and some grated Gruyère.

COOK'S TIP

Any firm fish can be used for this recipe. If you use whole fish, include the heads, which enhance the flavour of the soup.

PÂTÉS AND TERRINES

Smoked Salmon Pâté

Making this pâté in individual ramekins wrapped in extra smoked salmon gives a really special presentation. Taste the mousse as you are making it as some people prefer more lemon juice and salt and pepper.

INGREDIENTS

Serves 4

350g/12oz thinly sliced smoked salmon
   (wild if possible)
150ml/¼ pint/⅔ cup double cream
finely grated rind and juice of 1 lemon
salt and ground black pepper
melba toast, to serve

1 Line four small ramekin dishes with clear film. Then line the dishes with 115g/4oz of the smoked salmon cut into strips long enough to flop over the edges.

2 In a food processor fitted with a metal blade, process the rest of the salmon with the double cream, lemon rind and juice, salt and plenty of pepper.

3 Pack the lined ramekins with the smoked salmon pâté and wrap over the loose strips of salmon. Cover with clear film and chill for 30 minutes. Invert on to plates; serve with melba toast.

Smoked Haddock Pâté

Arbroath smokies are small haddock that are beheaded and gutted but not split before being salted and hot-smoked, creating a great flavour.

Serves 6

3 large Arbroath smokies, about
    225g/8oz each
275g/10oz/1¼ cups medium-fat
    soft cheese
3 eggs, beaten
30–45ml/2–3 tbsp lemon juice
ground black pepper
chervil sprigs, to garnish
lemon wedges and lettuce leaves, to serve

1 Preheat the oven to 160°C/
325°F/Gas 3. Butter six
ramekin dishes.

2 Lay the smokies in a baking
dish and heat through in the
oven for 10 minutes. Carefully
remove the skin and bones from
the smokies, then flake the flesh
into a bowl.

3 Mash the fish with a fork and
work in the cheese, then the
eggs. Add lemon juice and pepper.

4 Divide the fish mixture among
the ramekins and place in a
roasting tin. Pour hot water into
the roasting tin to come halfway
up the dishes. Bake for 30 minutes,
until just set.

5 Allow to cool for 2–3 minutes,
then run a knife point around
the edge of each dish and invert on
to a warmed plate. Garnish with
chervil sprigs and serve with the
lemon wedges and lettuce.

Chicken Liver Pâté

This rich-tasting, smooth pâté will keep in the fridge for about 3 days. Serve with thick slices of hot toast or warmed bread – a rustic olive oil bread such as ciabatta would be a good partner.

INGREDIENTS

Serves 8

115g/4oz chicken livers, thawed if frozen, trimmed

1 small garlic clove, chopped

15ml/1 tbsp sherry

30ml/2 tbsp brandy

50g/2oz/¼ cup butter, melted

2.5ml/¼ tsp salt

fresh herbs and black peppercorns, to garnish

hot toast or warmed bread, to serve

1 Preheat the oven to 150°C/ 300°F/Gas 2. Place the chicken livers and chopped garlic in a food processor or blender and process until they are smooth.

2 With the motor running, gradually add the sherry, brandy, melted butter and salt.

3 Pour the liver mixture into two 7.5cm/3in ramekins. Cover the tops with foil but do not allow the foil to come down the sides too far.

4 Place the ramekins in a small roasting pan and pour in boiling water so that it comes about halfway up the sides of the ramekins.

5 Carefully transfer the pan to the oven and bake the pâté for 20 minutes. Leave to cool to room temperature, then remove the ramekins from the pan and chill until needed. Serve the pâté with toast or bread, garnished with herbs and peppercorns.

Herbed Liver Pâté Pie

Serve this highly flavoured pâté with a glass of Pilsner beer for a change from wine.

INGREDIENTS

Serves 10

675g/1½ lb minced pork
350g/12oz pork liver
350g/12oz/2 cups diced cooked ham
1 small onion, finely chopped
30ml/2 tbsp chopped fresh parsley
5ml/1 tsp German mustard
30ml/2 tbsp Kirsch
5ml/1 tsp salt
beaten egg, for sealing and glazing
25g/1oz sachet aspic jelly
250ml/8fl oz/1 cup boiling water
ground black pepper
mustard, bread and dill pickles, to serve

For the pastry
450g/1lb/4 cups plain flour
pinch of salt
275g/10oz/1¼ cups butter
2 eggs plus 1 egg yolk
30ml/2 tbsp water

1 Preheat the oven to 200°C/400°F/Gas 6. To make the pastry, sift the flour and salt and rub in the butter. Beat the eggs, egg yolk and water, add to the dry ingredients and mix.

2 Knead the dough briefly until smooth. Roll out two-thirds on a lightly floured surface and use to line a 10 x 25cm/4 x 10in hinged loaf tin. Trim any excess dough.

3 Process half the pork and all of the liver until fairly smooth. Stir in the remaining minced pork, ham, onion, parsley, mustard, Kirsch, salt and black pepper to taste.

4 Spoon the filling into the tin, smoothing it down and then levelling the surface.

5 Roll out the remaining pastry on the lightly floured surface and use it to top the pie, sealing the edges with some of the beaten egg. Decorate with the pastry trimmings and glaze with the remaining beaten egg. Using a fork, make 3 or 4 holes in the top, for the steam to escape.

6 Bake for 40 minutes, then reduce the oven temperature to 180°C/350°F/Gas 4 and cook for a further hour. Cover the pastry with foil if the top begins to brown too much. Allow the pie to cool in the tin.

7 Make up the aspic jelly, using the boiling water. Stir to dissolve, then allow to cool.

8 Make a small hole near the edge of the pie with a skewer, then pour in the aspic through a greaseproof paper funnel. Chill for at least 2 hours before serving the pie in slices with mustard, bread and dill pickles.

Prawn, Egg and Avocado Mousses

A light and creamy mousse with lots of chunky texture and a great mix of flavours. Serve on the same day you make it but chill really well first.

INGREDIENTS

Serves 6

a little olive oil

1 sachet gelatine

juice and rind of 1 lemon

60ml/4 tbsp good-quality mayonnaise

60ml/4 tbsp chopped fresh dill

5ml/1 tsp anchovy essence

5ml/1 tsp Worcestershire sauce

1 large avocado, ripe but just firm

4 hard-boiled eggs, peeled and chopped

175g/6oz/1 cup cooked prawns (roughly
    chopped if large)

250ml/8fl oz/1 cup double or whipping
    cream, lightly whipped

2 egg whites, whisked

salt and ground black pepper

dill or parsley sprigs, to garnish

warmed granary bread or toast, to serve

1 Prepare six small ramekins. Lightly grease the dishes with olive oil, then wrap a greaseproof paper collar around the top of each and secure with tape. This ensures that you can fill the dishes as high as you like, and the extra mixture will be supported while setting and it will look really dramatic when you remove the paper. Alternatively, prepare just one small soufflé dish.

2 Dissolve the gelatine in the lemon juice with 15ml/1 tbsp hot water in a small bowl set over hot water, until clear, stirring occasionally. Allow to cool slightly then blend in the lemon rind, mayonnaise, dill and and anchovy essence and Worcestershire sauce.

3 In a medium bowl mash the avocado; add the eggs and prawns. Stir in the gelatine mixture and then fold in the cream, egg whites and seasoning to taste. When evenly blended spoon into the ramekins or soufflé dish and chill for 3–4 hours. Garnish with the herbs and serve with bread or toast.

COOK'S TIP

Other fish can make a good alternative to prawns. Try substituting the same quantity of smoked trout or salmon, or cooked crab meat.

Sea Trout Mousse

*This deliciously creamy mousse
makes a little sea trout go a long
way. It is equally good made
with salmon if sea trout is
unavailable. Serve with crisp
melba toast or triangles of lightly
toasted pitta bread.*

INGREDIENTS

Serves 6

250g/9oz sea trout fillet

120ml/4fl oz/½ cup fish stock

2 gelatine leaves, or 15ml/1 tbsp powdered
    gelatine

juice of ½ lemon

30ml/2 tbsp dry sherry or dry vermouth

30ml/2 tbsp freshly grated Parmesan

300ml/½ pint/1¼ cups whipping cream

2 egg whites

15ml/1 tbsp sunflower oil, for greasing

salt and ground white pepper

For the garnish

5cm/2in piece cucumber, with peel, thinly
    sliced and halved

fresh dill or chervil

1 Put the sea trout in a shallow
pan. Pour in the fish stock and
heat to simmering point. Poach
the fish for about 3–4 minutes,
until it is lightly cooked. Strain the
stock into a jug and leave the trout
to cool slightly.

2 Add the gelatine to the hot
stock and stir until it has
dissolved completely. Set aside
until required.

3 When the trout is cool enough
to handle, remove the skin and
flake the flesh. Pour the stock into a
food processor or blender. Process
briefly, then gradually add the
flaked trout, lemon juice, sherry or
vermouth and Parmesan through
the feeder tube, continuing to
process the mixture until it is
smooth. Scrape into a large bowl
and leave to cool completely.

4 Lightly whip the cream in a
bowl; fold it into the cold trout
mixture. Season to taste, then
cover with clear film and chill in
the fridge until the mousse is just
starting to set. It should have the
consistency of mayonnaise.

5 In a grease-free bowl, beat the
egg whites with a pinch of salt
until they are softly peaking. Then
using a large metal spoon, stir
about one-third of the egg whites
into the sea trout mixture to
slacken it slightly, then fold in
the rest.

6 Lightly grease six ramekins or
similar individual serving
dishes. Divide the mousse among
the prepared dishes and level the
surface. Place in the fridge for 2–3
hours, until set. Just before serving,
arrange a few slices of cucumber
and a small herb sprig on top of
each mousse and scatter over a
little chopped dill or chervil too.

Salmon Rillettes

This is an economical way of serving salmon, with only a little fillet required per head.

INGREDIENTS

Serves 6

350g/12oz salmon fillets
175g/6oz/¾ cup butter, softened
1 celery stick, finely chopped
1 leek, white part only, finely chopped
1 bay leaf
150ml/¼ pint/⅔ cup dry white wine
115g/4oz smoked salmon trimmings
generous pinch of ground mace
60ml/4 tbsp fromage frais
salt and ground black pepper
salad leaves, to serve

1 Lightly season the salmon. Melt 25g/1oz/2 tbsp of the butter in a medium sauté pan. Add the celery and leek and cook for about 5 minutes. Add the salmon and bay leaf and pour the white wine over. Cover and cook for about 15 minutes until tender.

2 Strain the cooking liquid into a pan and boil until reduced to 30ml/2 tbsp. Cool. Meanwhile, melt 50g/2oz/4 tbsp of the remaining butter and gently cook the smoked salmon trimmings until it turns pale pink. Leave to cool.

3 Remove the skin and any bones from the salmon fillets. Flake the flesh into a bowl and add the reduced, cooled cooking liquid.

4 Beat in the remaining butter, with the ground mace and the fromage frais. Break up the cooked smoked salmon trimmings and fold into the salmon mixture with all the juices from the pan. Taste and adjust the seasoning if you need to.

5 Spoon the salmon mixture into a dish or terrine and smooth the top level. Cover with clear film and chill. The prepared mixture can be left in the fridge for up to 2 days.

6 To serve the salmon rillettes, shape the mixture into oval quenelles using two dessert spoons and arrange on individual plates with the salad leaves. Accompany the rillettes with brown bread or oatcakes, if you like.

Brandade of Salt Cod

There are almost as many versions of this creamy salt cod purée as there are regions of France. Some contain mashed potatoes, others truffles. This comparatively light recipe includes garlic, but you can omit it and serve the brandade on toasted slices of French bread rubbed with garlic if you prefer.

INGREDIENTS

Serves 6

200g/7oz salt cod

250ml/8fl oz/1 cup extra virgin olive oil

4 garlic cloves, crushed

250ml/8fl oz/1 cup whipping or
  double cream

ground white pepper

shredded spring onions, to garnish

herbed crispbread, to serve

1 Soak the fish in cold water for 24 hours, changing the water often. Drain. Cut into pieces, place in a shallow pan and pour in cold water to cover. Heat the water until simmering, then poach the fish for 8 minutes, until it is just cooked. Drain, then remove the skin and bone the cod carefully.

2 Combine the olive oil and garlic in a small saucepan and heat to just below boiling point. In another saucepan, heat the cream until it starts to simmer.

3 Put the cod into a food processor, process it briefly, then gradually add alternate amounts of the garlic-flavoured olive oil and cream, while keeping the machine running.

4 Once the mixture has the consistency of mashed potatoes add white pepper to taste, then scoop the branade into a serving bowl. Garnish with shredded spring onions and serve warm with herbed crispbread.

COOK'S TIP
~
You can purée the fish mixture in a mortar with a pestle. This gives a better texture, but is notoriously hard work.

Potted Salmon with Lemon and Dill

This sophisticated starter would be ideal for a dinner party. Preparation is done well in advance, so you can concentrate on the main course, or if you are really well organized, you can enjoy a pre-dinner conversation with your guests. If you cannot find fresh dill use 5ml/1 tsp dried dill instead.

INGREDIENTS

Serves 6

350g/12oz cooked salmon, skinned
150g/5oz/⅔ cup butter, softened
rind and juice of 1 large lemon
10ml/2 tsp chopped fresh dill
salt and ground white pepper
75g/3oz/¾ cup flaked almonds,
    roughly chopped

1 Flake the salmon into a bowl and then place in a food processor together with two-thirds of the butter, the lemon rind and juice, half the dill, and plenty of salt and pepper. Blend until the mixture is quite smooth.

2 Mix in the flaked almonds. Check the seasoning and pack the mixture into small ramekins.

3 Scatter the other half of the dill over the top of each ramekin. Clarify the remaining butter, and pour over each ramekin to make a seal. Chill. Serve with crudités.

Potted Prawns

The tiny brown prawns that were traditionally used for potting are very fiddly to peel. Since they are rare nowadays, it is easier to use peeled cooked prawns instead.

INGREDIENTS

Serves 4

225g/8oz/2 cups shelled prawns

225g/8oz/1 cup butter

pinch of ground mace

salt, to taste

cayenne pepper

dill sprigs, to garnish

lemon wedges and thin slices of brown
   bread and butter, to serve

1 Chop a quarter of the prawns. Melt 115g/4oz/½ cup of the butter slowly, carefully skimming off any foam that rises to the surface with a metal spoon.

2 Stir all the prawns, the mace, salt and cayenne into the pan and heat gently without boiling. Pour the prawns and butter mixture into four individual pots and leave to cool.

3 Heat the remaining butter in a clean small saucepan, then carefully spoon the clear butter over the prawns, leaving behind the sediment.

4 Leave until the butter is almost set, then place a dill sprig in the centre of each pot. Leave to set completely, then cover and chill.

5 Transfer the prawns to room temperature 30 minutes before serving with lemon wedges for squeezing over and thin slices of brown bread and butter.

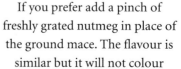

COOK'S TIP

If you prefer add a pinch of freshly grated nutmeg in place of the ground mace. The flavour is similar but it will not colour the dish.

Grilled Vegetable Terrine

A colourful, layered terrine, this starter uses all the vegetables that are associated with the Mediterranean and long, balmy summer evenings.

INGREDIENTS

Serves 6

2 large red peppers, quartered, cored
   and seeded
2 large yellow peppers, quartered, cored
   and seeded
1 large aubergine, sliced lengthways
2 large courgettes, sliced lengthways
90ml/6 tbsp olive oil
1 large red onion, thinly sliced
75g/3oz/½ cup raisins
15ml/1 tbsp tomato purée
15ml/1 tbsp red wine vinegar
400ml/14fl oz/1⅔ cups tomato juice
15g/½oz/2 tbsp powdered gelatine
fresh basil leaves, to garnish

For the dressing
90ml/6 tbsp extra virgin olive oil
30ml/2 tbsp red wine vinegar
salt and ground black pepper

1 Place the prepared peppers skin side up under a hot grill and cook until the skins are blackened. Transfer to a bowl and cover with a plate. Leave to cool.

2 Arrange the aubergine and courgette slices on separate baking sheets. Brush them with a little oil and cook under the grill, turning occasionally, until they are tender and golden.

3 Heat the remaining olive oil in a frying pan, and add the sliced onion, raisins, tomato purée and red wine vinegar. Cook gently until the mixture is soft and syrupy. Set aside and leave to cool in the frying pan.

4 Line a 1.75 litre/3 pint/7½ cup terrine with clear film, (it helps if you lightly oil the terrine first) leaving a little hanging over the sides of the container.

5 Pour half the tomato juice into a saucepan, and sprinkle with the gelatine. Dissolve gently over a low heat, stirring to prevent any lumps from forming.

6 Place a layer of red peppers in the base of the terrine, and pour in enough of the tomato juice with gelatine to cover.

7 Continue layering the vegetables, pouring tomato juice over each layer. Finishing with a layer of red peppers. Add the remaining tomato juice to the pan, and pour into the terrine. Give it a sharp tap, to disperse the juice. Cover and chill until set.

8 To make the dressing, whisk together the oil and vinegar, and season. Turn out the terrine and remove the clear film. Serve in thick slices, drizzled with dressing and garnished with basil leaves.

COOK'S TIP

Ring the changes and use orange and green peppers along with or in place of the red and yellow ones. French beans, simply boiled first, would make a nice addition, as would a layer of peas or sweetcorn.

Roast Pepper Terrine

This terrine is perfect for a dinner party because it tastes better if made ahead. Prepare the salsa on the day of serving. Serve with a warmed Italian bread such as ciabatta or the flavoursome focaccia.

INGREDIENTS

Serves 8

8 peppers (red, yellow and orange)

675g/1½ lb/3 cups mascarpone cheese

3 eggs, separated

30ml/2 tbsp each roughly chopped flat leaf parsley and shredded basil

2 large garlic cloves, roughly chopped

2 red, yellow or orange peppers, seeded and roughly chopped

30ml/2 tbsp extra virgin olive oil

10ml/2 tsp balsamic vinegar

a few basil sprigs

salt and ground black pepper

1 Place the whole peppers under a hot grill for 8–10 minutes, turning frequently. Then put into a polythene bag until cold before skinning and seeding them. Chop seven of the peppers lengthways into thin strips.

2 Put the mascarpone cheese in a bowl with the egg yolks, herbs and half the garlic. Add salt and pepper to taste. Beat well. In a separate bowl, whisk the egg whites to a soft peak, then fold into the cheese mixture until they are evenly incorporated.

3 Preheat the oven to 180°C/ 350°F/Gas 4. Line the base of a lightly oiled 900g/2lb loaf tin. Put one-third of the cheese mixture in the tin and spread level. Arrange half the pepper strips on top in an even layer. Repeat until all the cheese and peppers are used, ending with a layer of the cheese mixture.

4 Cover the tin with foil and place in a roasting tin. Pour in boiling water to come halfway up the sides of the tin. Bake for 1 hour. Leave to cool in the water bath, then lift out and chill overnight.

5 A few hours before serving, make the salsa. Place the remaining skinned pepper and fresh peppers in a food processor. Add the remaining garlic, oil and vinegar. Set aside a few basil leaves for garnishing and add the rest to the processor. Process until finely chopped. Tip the mixture into a bowl, add salt and pepper to taste and mix well. Cover and chill until ready to serve.

6 Turn out the terrine, peel off the lining paper and slice thickly. Garnish with the reserved basil leaves and serve cold, with the sweet pepper salsa.

Asparagus and Egg Terrine

For a special dinner this terrine is a delicious choice yet it is very light. Make the hollandaise sauce well in advance and warm through gently when required.

Serves 8

150ml/¼ pint/⅔ cup milk

150ml/¼ pint/⅔ cup double cream

40g/1½oz/3 tbsp butter

40g/1½oz/3 tbsp flour

75g/3oz herbed or garlic cream cheese

675g/1½ lb asparagus spears, cooked

a little oil

2 eggs, separated

15ml/1 tbsp snipped fresh chives

30ml/2 tbsp chopped fresh dill

salt and ground black pepper

dill sprigs, to garnish

For the orange hollandaise sauce

15ml/1 tbsp white wine vinegar

15ml/1 tbsp fresh orange juice

4 black peppercorns

1 bay leaf

2 egg yolks

115g/4oz/½ cup butter, melted and
    cooled slightly

1 Put the milk and cream into a small saucepan and heat to just below boiling point. Melt the butter in a medium pan, stir in the flour and cook to a thick paste. Gradually stir in the milk, whisking as it thickens and beat to a smooth paste. Stir in the cream cheese, season to taste with salt and ground black pepper and leave to cool slightly.

2 Trim the asparagus to fit the width of a 1.2 litre/2 pint/ 5 cup bread tin or terrine. Lightly oil the tin and then place a sheet of greaseproof paper in the base, cut to fit. Preheat the oven to 180°C/ 350°F/Gas 4.

3 Beat the yolks into the sauce mixture. Whisk the whites until stiff and fold in with the chives, dill and seasoning. Layer the asparagus and egg mixture in the tin, starting and finishing with asparagus. Cover the top with foil.

4 Place the terrine in a roasting tin; half fill with hot water. Cook for 45–55 minutes until firm.

5 To make the sauce, put the vinegar, juice, peppercorns and bay leaf in a small pan and heat until reduced by half.

6 Cool the sauce slightly, then whisk in the egg yolks, then the butter, with a balloon whisk over a very gentle heat. Season to taste and keep whisking until thick. Keep the sauce warm over a pan of hot water.

7 When the terrine is just firm to the touch remove from the oven and allow to cool, then chill. Carefully invert the terrine on to a serving dish, remove the grease-proof paper and garnish with the dill. Cut into slices and pour over the warmed sauce.

Haddock and Smoked Salmon Terrine

This is a fairly substantial terrine so serve modest slices, perhaps accompanied by fresh dill mayonnaise or a fresh mango salsa. Follow with a light main course and a fruit-based dessert.

INGREDIENTS

Serves 10–12

15ml/1 tbsp sunflower oil,
    for greasing
350g/12oz oak-smoked salmon
900g/2lb haddock fillets, skinned
2 eggs, lightly beaten
105ml/7 tbsp crème fraîche
30ml/2 tbsp drained capers
30ml/2 tbsp drained soft green or
    pink peppercorns
salt and ground white pepper
crème fraîche, peppercorns and fresh dill
    and rocket, to garnish

1 Preheat the oven to 200°C/400°F/Gas 6. Grease a 1 litre/1¾ pint/4 cup loaf tin or terrine with the sunflower oil. Use some of the smoked salmon to line the loaf tin or terrine, allowing some of the ends to overhang the mould. Reserve the remaining smoked salmon until needed.

2 Cut two long slices of haddock the length of the tin or terrine and set aside. Cut the rest of the haddock into small pieces. Season all of the haddock with salt and ground white pepper.

3 Combine the eggs, crème fraîche, capers and green or pink peppercorns in a bowl. Add salt and pepper; stir in the haddock pieces. Spoon the mixture into the mould until it is one-third full. Smooth the surface with a spatula.

4 Wrap the long haddock fillets in the reserved salmon. Lay them on top of the layer of the fish mixture in the tin or terrine.

5 Cover with the rest of the fish mixture, smooth the surface and fold the overhanging pieces of salmon over the top. Cover tightly with a double thickness of foil. Tap the terrine to settle the contents.

6 Stand the terrine in a roasting tin and pour in boiling water to come halfway up the sides. Place in the oven and cook for 45 minutes–1 hour, until the filling is just set.

7 Take the terrine out of the roasting tin, but do not remove the foil cover. Place two or three large heavy tins on the foil to weight it and leave until cold. Chill in the fridge for 24 hours.

8 About an hour before serving, remove the terrine from the fridge, lift off the weights and remove the foil. Carefully invert on to a serving plate and garnish with crème fraîche, peppercorns and sprigs of dill and rocket leaves.

COOK'S TIP

Use any thick white fish fillets for this terrine; try cod, whiting, hake or hoki.

Striped Fish Terrine

Serve this terrine cold or just warm, with a hollandaise sauce if you like.

INGREDIENTS

Serves 8

15ml/1 tbsp sunflower oil

450g/1lb salmon fillet, skinned

450g/1lb sole fillets, skinned

3 egg whites

105ml/7 tbsp double cream

15ml/1 tbsp finely snipped fresh chives

juice of 1 lemon

115g/4oz/scant 1 cup fresh or frozen
    peas, cooked

5ml/1 tsp chopped fresh mint

salt, ground white pepper and
    grated nutmeg

thinly sliced cucumber, salad cress and
    whole chives, to garnish

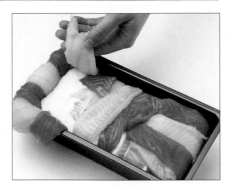

1 Grease a 1 litre/1¾ pint/4 cup loaf tin or terrine with the oil. Slice the salmon thinly; cut it and the sole into long strips, 2.5cm/1in wide. Preheat the oven to 200°C/400°F/Gas 6.

2 Line the terrine neatly with alternate slices of salmon and sole leaving the ends overhanging the edge. You should be left with about a third of the salmon and half the sole.

3 In a grease-free bowl, beat the egg whites with a pinch of salt until they form soft peaks. Purée the remaining sole in a food processor. Spoon into a mixing bowl, season, then fold in two-thirds of the egg whites, followed by two-thirds of the cream. Put half the mixture into a second bowl; stir in the chives. Add nutmeg to the first bowl.

4 Purée the remaining salmon, scrape it into a bowl; add the lemon juice. Fold in the remaining egg whites, then the remaining cream.

5 Purée the peas with the mint. Season the mixture and spread it over the base of the terrine, smoothing the surface with a spatula. Spoon over the sole with chives mixture and spread evenly.

6 Add the salmon mixture, then finish with the plain sole mixture. Cover with the overhanging fish fillets and make a lid of oiled foil. Stand the terrine in a roasting tin and pour in enough boiling water to come halfway up the sides.

7 Bake for 15–20 minutes, until the top fillets are just cooked and the mousse feels springy. Remove the foil, lay a wire rack over the top of the terrine and invert both rack and terrine on to a lipped baking sheet to catch the cooking juices that drain out. Keep these to make fish stock or soup.

8 Leaving the tin in place, let the terrine stand for about 15 minutes, then turn it over again, invert it on to a serving dish and lift off the tin carefully. Serve warm, or chill in the fridge first and serve cold. Garnish with thinly sliced cucumber, salad cress and chives before serving.

Turkey, Juniper and Peppercorn Terrine

This is an ideal dish for entertaining, as it can be made several days in advance. If you prefer, arrange some of the pancetta and pistachio nuts as a layer in the middle of the terrine.

INGREDIENTS

Serves 10–12

225g/8oz chicken livers, trimmed

450g/1lb minced turkey

450g/11b minced pork

225g/8oz cubetti pancetta

50g/2oz/½ cup shelled pistachio nuts, roughly chopped

5ml/1 tsp salt

2.5ml/½ tsp ground mace

2 garlic cloves, crushed

5ml/1 tsp drained green peppercorns in brine

5ml/1 tsp juniper berries

120ml/4fl oz/½ cup dry white wine

30ml/2 tbsp gin

finely grated rind of 1 orange

8 large vacuum-packed vine leaves in brine

oil, for greasing

1 Chop the chicken livers finely. Put them in a bowl and add the turkey, pork, pancetta, pistachio nuts, salt, mace and garlic. Mix well.

2 Lightly crush the peppercorns and juniper berries and add them to the mixture. Stir in the white wine, gin and orange rind. Cover and chill overnight to allow the flavours to mingle.

3 Preheat the oven to 160°C/ 325°F/Gas 3. Rinse the vine leaves under cold running water. Drain them thoroughly. Lightly oil a 1.2 litre/2 pint/5 cup pâté terrine or loaf tin. Line the terrine or tin with the leaves, letting the ends hang over the sides. Pack the mixture into the terrine or tin and fold the leaves over to enclose the filling. Brush lightly with oil.

4 Cover the terrine with its lid or with foil. Place it in a roasting tin and pour in boiling water to come halfway up the sides of the terrine. Bake for 1¾ hours, checking the level of the water occasionally, so that the roasting tin does not dry out.

5 Leave the terrine to cool, then pour off the surface juices. Cover with clear film, then foil and place weights on top. Chill in the fridge overnight. Serve at room temperature with a pickle or chutney such as spiced kumquats or red pepper and chilli jelly.

Chicken and Pork Terrine

This pale, elegant terrine is flecked with green peppercorns and parsley which give it a wonderfully subtle flavour.

INGREDIENTS

Serves 6–8

225g/8oz rindless, streaky bacon

375g/13oz boneless chicken breast, skinned

15ml/1 tbsp lemon juice

225g/8oz lean minced pork

½ small onion, finely chopped

2 eggs, beaten

30ml/2 tbsp chopped fresh parsley

5ml/1 tsp salt

5ml/1 tsp green peppercorns, crushed

oil, for greasing

salad leaves, radishes and lemon wedges, to serve

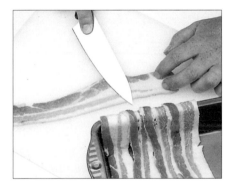

1 Preheat the oven to 160°C/ 325°F/Gas 3. Put the bacon on a board and stretch it using the back of a knife before arranging it in overlapping slices over the base and sides of a 900g/2lb loaf tin.

2 Cut 115g/4oz of the chicken into strips about 10cm/4in long. Sprinkle with lemon juice. Put the rest of the chicken in a food processor or blender with the minced pork and the onion. Process until fairly smooth.

3 Add the eggs, parsley, salt and peppercorns to the meat mixture and process again briefly. Spoon half the mixture into the loaf tin and then level the surface.

4 Arrange the chicken strips on top, then spoon in the remaining meat mixture and smooth the top. Give the tin a couple of sharp taps to knock out any pockets of air.

5 Cover the loaf tin with a piece of oiled foil and put it in a roasting tin. Pour in enough hot water to come halfway up the sides of the loaf tin. Bake for about 45–50 minutes, until firm.

6 Allow the terrine to cool in the tin before turning out and chilling. Serve sliced, with salad leaves, radishes and wedges of lemon for squeezing.

COOK'S TIP

For a slightly sharper flavour, substitute chopped fresh coriander for the parsley. It goes well with the lemon.

VEGETARIAN

Potato Skewers with Mustard Dip

Potatoes cooked on the barbecue have a great flavour and crisp skin. Try these delicious kebabs served with a thick, garlic-rich dip for an unusual start to a meal.

INGREDIENTS

Serves 6

For the dip

4 garlic cloves, crushed

2 egg yolks

30ml/2 tbsp lemon juice

300ml/½ pint/1¼ cups extra virgin olive oil

10ml/2 tsp wholegrain mustard

salt and ground black pepper

For the skewers

1kg/2¼ lb small new potatoes

200g/7oz shallots, halved

30ml/2 tbsp olive oil

15ml/1 tbsp sea salt

1 Prepare the barbecue. Preheat the grill. To make the dip place the garlic, egg yolks and lemon juice in a blender or a food processor fitted with a metal blade and process for just a few seconds until the mixture is smooth.

2 Keep the blender motor running and add the oil very gradually, pouring it in a thin stream, until the mixture forms a thick, glossy cream. Add the mustard and stir the ingredients together, then season with salt and pepper. Chill until ready to use.

3 Par-boil the potatoes in their skins in boiling water for 5 minutes. Drain well and then thread them on to metal skewers alternating with the shallots.

4 Brush the skewers with oil and sprinkle with salt. Barbecue or grill for about 10–12 minutes, turning occasionally. Serve with the mustard dip.

COOK'S TIP

Only early or "new" potatoes and salad potatoes have the firmness necessary to stay on the skewer.

Griddled Tomatoes on Soda Bread

Nothing could be simpler than this delightful appetizer, yet a drizzle of olive oil and balsamic vinegar and shavings of Parmesan cheese transform it into something really rather special.

INGREDIENTS

Serves 4

olive oil, for brushing and drizzling

6 tomatoes, thickly sliced

4 thick slices soda bread

balsamic vinegar, for drizzling

salt and ground black pepper

shavings of Parmesan cheese, to serve

1 Brush a griddle pan with olive oil and heat. Add the tomato slices and cook them for about 4 minutes, turning once, until softened and slightly blackened. Alternatively, heat the grill to high and line the rack with foil. Grill the tomato slices for 4–6 minutes, turning once, until softened.

2 Meanwhile, lightly toast the soda bread. Place the tomatoes on top of the toast and drizzle each portion with a little olive oil and balsamic vinegar. Season to taste and serve immediately with thin shavings of Parmesan cheese.

COOK'S TIP

Using a griddle pan reduces the amount of oil required for cooking the tomatoes which is useful for those watching their weight. It also gives them a delicious barbecued flavour.

Marinated Feta Cheese with Capers

Marinating cubes of feta cheese with herbs and spices gives a marvellous flavour. Serve with toast.

INGREDIENTS

Serves 6

350g/12oz feta cheese

2 garlic cloves

2.5ml/½ tsp mixed peppercorns

8 coriander seeds

1 bay leaf

15–30ml/1–2 tbsp drained capers

oregano or thyme sprigs

olive oil, to cover

hot toast, to serve

1 Cut the feta cheese into cubes. Thickly slice the garlic. Put the mixed peppercorns and coriander seeds in a mortar and crush lightly with a pestle.

2 Pack the feta cubes into a large preserving jar with the bay leaf, interspersing layers of cheese with garlic, crushed peppercorns and coriander, capers and the fresh oregano or thyme sprigs.

3 Pour in enough olive oil to cover the cheese. Close tightly and leave to marinate for two weeks in the fridge.

4 Lift out the feta cubes and serve on hot toast, with some chopped tomatoes and a little of the flavoured oil from the jar drizzled over.

COOK'S TIP

Add stoned black or green olives to the feta cheese in the marinade if you like.

Cannellini Bean and Rosemary Bruschetta

This variation on the theme of beans on toast makes an unusual but sophisticated starter.

Serves 6

150g/5oz/⅔ cup dried cannellini beans

5 tomatoes

45ml/3 tbsp olive oil, plus extra
    for drizzling

2 sun-dried tomatoes in oil, drained and
    finely chopped

1 garlic clove, crushed

30ml/2 tbsp chopped fresh rosemary

12 slices Italian-style bread, such
    as ciabatta

1 large garlic clove

salt and ground black pepper

handful of fresh basil leaves, to garnish

1 Put the beans in a bowl, cover in water and soak overnight. Drain and rinse the beans, then place in a saucepan and cover with fresh water. Bring to the boil and boil rapidly for 10 minutes. Then simmer for 50–60 minutes or until tender. Drain, return to the pan and keep warm.

2 Meanwhile, place the tomatoes in a bowl, cover with boiling water; leave for 30 seconds, then peel, seed and chop the flesh. Heat the oil in a frying pan, add the fresh and sun-dried tomatoes, garlic and rosemary. Cook for 2 minutes until the tomatoes begin to break down and soften.

3 Add the tomato mixture to the cannellini beans and season to taste. Mix together well. Keep the bean mixture warm.

4 Rub the cut sides of the bread slices with the garlic clove, then toast them lightly. Spoon the cannellini bean mixture on top of the toast. Sprinkle with basil leaves and drizzle with a little extra olive oil before serving.

Greek Aubergine and Spinach Pie

Aubergines layered with spinach, feta cheese and rice make a flavoursome and dramatic filling for a pie. It can be served warm or cold in elegant slices.

INGREDIENTS

Serves 12

375g/13oz shortcrust pastry, thawed
   if frozen
45–60ml/3–4 tbsp olive oil
1 large aubergine, sliced into rounds
1 onion, chopped
1 garlic clove, crushed
175g/6oz spinach, washed
4 eggs
75g/3oz/½ cup crumbled feta cheese
40g/1½oz/½ cup freshly grated
   Parmesan cheese
60ml/4 tbsp natural yogurt
90ml/6 tbsp creamy milk
225g/8oz/2 cups cooked white or brown
   long grain rice
salt and ground black pepper

2 Heat 30–45ml/2–3 tbsp of the oil in a frying pan and fry the aubergine slices for 6–8 minutes on each side until golden. You may need to add a little more oil at first, but this will be released as the flesh softens. Lift out and drain well on kitchen paper.

3 Add the onion and garlic to the oil remaining in the pan then fry over a gentle heat for 4–5 minutes until soft, adding a little extra oil if necessary.

4 Chop the spinach finely, by hand or in a food processor. Beat the eggs in a large mixing bowl, then add the spinach, feta, Parmesan, yogurt, milk and the onion mixture. Season well with salt and ground black pepper and stir thoroughly to mix.

5 Spread the rice in an even layer over the base of the part-baked pastry case. Reserve a few aubergine slices for the top, and arrange the rest in an even layer over the rice.

6 Spoon the spinach and feta mixture over the aubergines and place the remaining slices on top. Bake for 30–40 minutes until lightly browned. Serve the pie while warm, or leave it to cool completely before transferring to a serving plate.

1 Preheat the oven to 180°C/ 350°F/Gas 4. Roll out the pastry thinly and use to line a 25cm/10in flan tin. Prick the base all over and bake in the oven for 10–12 minutes until the pastry is pale golden. (Alternatively, bake blind, having lined the pastry with baking parchment and weighted it with a handful of baking beans.)

COOK'S TIP

Courgettes could be used in place of the aubergines, if you prefer. Fry the sliced courgettes in a little oil for 3–4 minutes until they are evenly golden. You will need to use three to four standard courgettes, or choose baby courgettes instead and slice them horizontally.

Glamorgan Sausages

These tasty sausages are ideal for vegetarians as they are made from cheese and leeks rather than meat.

INGREDIENTS

Makes 8

150g/5oz/2½ cups fresh breadcrumbs

150g/5oz generous cup grated Caerphilly cheese

1 small leek, very finely chopped

15ml/1 tbsp chopped fresh parsley

leaves from 1 thyme sprig, chopped

2 eggs

7.5ml/1½ tsp English mustard powder

about 45ml/3 tbsp milk

plain flour, for coating

15ml/1 tbsp oil

15g/½ oz/1 tbsp butter, melted

salt and ground black pepper

salad leaves and tomato halves, to serve

1 Mix the breadcrumbs, cheese, leek, herbs and seasoning. Whisk the eggs with the mustard and reserve 30ml/2 tbsp. Stir the rest into the cheese mixture with enough milk to bind.

2 Divide the cheese mixture into eight portions and form into sausage shapes.

3 Dip the sausages in the reserved egg to coat. Season the flour, then roll the sausages in it to give a light, even coating. Chill for about 30 minutes until firm.

4 Preheat the grill and oil the grill rack. Mix the oil and melted butter together and use to brush over the sausages. Grill the sausages for 5–10 minutes, turning them carefully every now and then, until golden brown all over. Serve hot or cold, with salad leaves and tomato halves.

Birds' Nests

A recipe from an old hand-written cookery book dated 1887. These are also known as Welsh Eggs because they resemble Scotch Eggs but they have leeks in the filling.

INGREDIENTS

Serves 6

6 eggs, hard-boiled

flour, seasoned with salt and paprika

1 leek, chopped

10ml/2 tsp sunflower oil

115g/4oz/2 cups fresh white breadcrumbs

grated rind and juice of 1 lemon

50g/2oz/½ cup vegetarian shredded suet

60ml/4 tbsp chopped fresh parsley

5ml/1 tsp dried thyme

salt and ground black pepper

1 egg, beaten

75g/3oz/½ cup dried breadcrumbs

oil, for deep-frying

lettuce and tomato wedges, to garnish

1 Peel the hard-boiled eggs and toss in the seasoned flour. Set aside until needed.

2 Fry the leeks in the sunflower oil for about 3 minutes until softened but not browned. Remove from the heat and leave to cool, then mix with the fresh breadcrumbs, lemon rind and juice, suet, herbs and salt and pepper. If the mixture is a bit too dry add a little water.

3 Shape the mixture around the eggs, moulding it firmly with your hands, then toss first into the beaten egg and then the dried breadcrumbs. Set aside on a plate to chill for 30 minutes. This will firm them up before cooking.

4 Pour enough oil to fill to one-third full a deep-fat fryer and heat to 190°C/375°F. Fry the eggs for about 3 minutes in two batches. Remove and drain on kitchen paper.

5 Serve cool, cut in half to reveal the "birds' nests", garnished with lettuce and tomato wedges.

Son-in-law Eggs

This fascinating name comes from a story about a prospective bridegroom who wanted to impress his future mother-in-law and devised a recipe from the only other dish he knew how to make – boiled eggs. The hard-boiled eggs are deep fried and then drenched with a sweet piquant tamarind sauce.

INGREDIENTS

Serves 4–6

75g/3oz/generous ⅓ cup palm sugar

60ml/4 tbsp light soy sauce

105ml/7 tbsp tamarind juice

oil, for frying

6 shallots, finely sliced

6 garlic cloves, finely sliced

6 red chillies, sliced

6 hard-boiled eggs, shelled

coriander sprigs, to garnish

lettuce, to serve

1 Combine the palm sugar, fish sauce and tamarind juice in a small saucepan. Bring to the boil, stirring until the sugar dissolves, then simmer the sauce for about 5 minutes.

2 Taste and add more palm sugar, fish sauce or tamarind juice, if necessary. It should be sweet, salty and slightly sour. Transfer the sauce to a bowl and set aside until needed.

3 Heat a couple of spoonfuls of the oil in a frying pan and fry the shallots, garlic and chillies until golden brown. Transfer the mixture to a bowl and set aside.

4 Deep-fry the eggs in hot oil for 3–5 minutes until golden brown. Drain on kitchen paper, quarter and arrange on a bed of lettuce. Scatter the shallot mixture over, drizzle with the sauce and garnish with coriander.

Dolmades

These stuffed vine leaves originated in Greece. If you can't locate fresh vine leaves, use a packet or can of brined leaves. Soak in hot water for 20 minutes, then rinse and dry well on kitchen paper before use.

INGREDIENTS

Makes 20 to 24

24–28 fresh young vine leaves, soaked

30ml/2 tbsp olive oil

1 large onion, finely chopped

1 garlic clove, crushed

225g/8oz/2 cups cooked long grain rice, or mixed white and wild rice

about 45ml/3 tbsp pine nuts

15ml/1 tbsp flaked almonds

40g/1½ oz/¼ cup sultanas

15ml/1 tbsp snipped fresh chives

15ml/1 tbsp finely chopped fresh mint

juice of ½ lemon

150ml/¼ pint/⅔ cup white wine

hot vegetable stock

salt and ground black pepper

mint sprig, to garnish

garlic yogurt and pitta bread, to serve

1 Bring a large pan of water to the boil and cook the vine leaves for about 2–3 minutes. They will darken and go limp after about 1 minute and simmering for a further minute or so will ensure they are pliable. If using packet or canned leaves, place in a bowl, cover with boiling water and leave for 20 minutes until the leaves can be separated easily. Rinse and dry on kitchen paper.

2 Heat the oil in a small frying pan and fry the onion and garlic for 3–4 minutes over a gentle heat until soft. Spoon the mixture into a large bowl and add the cooked rice. Stir to combine.

3 Stir in 30ml/2 tbsp of the pine nuts, the almonds, sultanas, chives and mint. Squeeze in the lemon juice. Add salt and pepper to taste and mix well.

4 Set aside four large vine leaves. Lay a vine leaf on a clean work surface, veined side uppermost. Place a spoonful of filling near the stem, fold the lower part of the vine leaf over it and roll up, folding in the sides as you go. Stuff the rest of the vine leaves in the same way.

5 Line the base of a deep frying pan with the reserved vine leaves. Place the dolmades close together in the pan, seam side down, in a single layer. Pour over the wine and enough stock to just cover. Anchor the dolmades by placing a plate on top of them, then cover the pan and simmer gently for 30 minutes.

6 Transfer the dolmades to a plate. Cool, chill, then garnish with the remaining pine nuts and the mint. Serve with a little garlic yogurt and some pitta bread.

Poached Eggs Florentine

The term "à la Florentine" means "in the style of Florence" and refers to dishes cooked with spinach and topped with mornay sauce. Here is a subtly spiced, elegant starter.

INGREDIENTS

Serves 4

675g/1½ lb spinach, washed and drained
25g/1oz/2 tbsp butter
60ml/4 tbsp double cream
pinch of freshly grated nutmeg
salt and ground black pepper

For the topping

25g/1oz/2 tbsp butter
25g/1oz/¼ cup plain flour
300ml/½ pint/1¼ cups hot milk
pinch of ground mace
115g/4oz Gruyère cheese, grated
4 eggs
15ml/1 tbsp freshly grated
   Parmesan cheese, plus shavings to serve

1 Place the spinach in a large pan with very little water. Cook for 3–4 minutes or until tender, then drain and chop finely. Return the spinach to the pan, add the butter, cream, nutmeg and seasoning and heat through. Place in the base of one large or four small gratin dishes.

2 To make the topping, heat the butter in a small pan, add the flour and cook for 1 minute to a paste. Gradually blend in the hot milk, beating well as it thickens to break up any lumps.

3 Cook for 1–2 minutes stirring. Remove from the heat and stir in the mace and three-quarters of the Gruyère cheese.

4 Preheat the oven to 200°C/400°F/Gas 6. Poach the eggs in lightly salted water for 3–4 minutes. Make hollows in the spinach with the back of a spoon, and place a poached egg in each one. Cover with the cheese sauce and sprinkle with the remaining Gruyère and Parmesan. Bake for 10 minutes or until golden. Serve at once with Parmesan shavings.

Chilli Cheese Tortilla with Tomato Salsa

Good warm or cold, this is like a quiche without the pastry base. Cheese and chillies are more than a match for each other.

INGREDIENTS

Serves 8

45ml/3 tbsp sunflower or olive oil
1 small onion, thinly sliced
2–3 green jalapeño chillies, sliced
200g/7oz cold cooked potato, thinly sliced
120g/4¼ oz/generous 1 cup grated
    Manchego, Mexican queso blanco or
    Monterey Jack cheese
6 eggs, beaten
salt and ground black pepper
fresh herbs, to garnish

For the salsa

500g/1¼ lb fresh flavoursome tomatoes,
    peeled, seeded and finely chopped
1 green chilli, seeded and finely chopped
2 garlic cloves, crushed
45ml/3 tbsp chopped fresh coriander
juice of 1 lime
2.5ml/½ tsp salt

1 Make the salsa. Put the tomatoes in a bowl with the rest of the ingredients. Mix well and set aside.

COOK'S TIP

If you cannot find the cheeses listed, use a medium Cheddar instead.

2 Heat half the oil in a large omelette pan and gently fry the onion and jalapeños for 5 minutes, stirring once or twice, until softened. Add the potato and cook for a further 5 minutes until lightly browned, taking care to keep the slices whole.

3 Using a slotted spoon, transfer the vegetables to a warm plate. Wipe the pan with kitchen paper, then pour in the remaining oil. Heat well and return the vegetable mixture to the pan. Scatter the cheese over the top.

4 Pour in the beaten egg, making sure that it seeps under the vegetables. Cook the tortilla over a gentle heat until set. Serve in wedges, garnished with fresh herbs, with the salsa on the side.

Baked Mediterranean Vegetables

Crisp and golden crunchy batter surrounds these vegetables, turning them into a substantial starter. Use other vegetables instead if you prefer.

INGREDIENTS

Serves 10–12

1 small aubergine, trimmed, halved and
    thickly sliced
1 egg
115g/4oz/1 cup plain flour
300ml/½ pint/1¼ cups milk
30ml/2 tbsp fresh thyme leaves, or
    10ml/2 tsp dried
1 red onion
2 large courgettes
1 red pepper
1 yellow pepper
60–75ml/4–5 tbsp sunflower oil
salt and ground black pepper
30ml/2 tbsp freshly grated
    Parmesan cheese and fresh herbs,
    to garnish

1 Place the aubergine in a colander or sieve, sprinkle generously with salt and leave for 10 minutes. Drain and pat dry on kitchen paper.

2 Meanwhile, to make the batter, beat the egg, then gradually beat in the flour and a little milk to make a smooth thick paste. Blend in the rest of the milk, add the thyme leaves and seasoning to taste and blend until smooth. Leave in a cool place until required.

3 Quarter the onion and slice the courgettes and seed and quarter the peppers. Put the oil in a roasting tin and heat through in the oven at 220°C/425°F/Gas 7. Add all the vegetables, turn in the fat to coat them well and return to the oven for 20 minutes until they start to cook.

4 Give the batter another whisk then pour over the vegetables and return to the oven for 30 minutes. If well puffed up and golden, then reduce the heat to 190°C/375°F/Gas 5 for another 10–15 minutes until crisp around the edges. Sprinkle with Parmesan and herbs and serve.

COOK'S TIP

It is essential to get the fat in the dish really hot before adding the batter, or it will not rise well. Use a dish which is not too deep.

Courgette Fritters with Chilli Jam

Chilli jam is hot, sweet and sticky – rather like a thick chutney. It adds a delicious piquancy to these light courgette fritters which are always a popular dish.

INGREDIENTS

Makes 12 Fritters

450g/1lb/3½ cups coarsely grated courgettes
50g/2oz/⅔ cup freshly grated Parmesan cheese
2 eggs, beaten
60ml/4 tbsp plain flour
vegetable oil, for frying
salt and ground black pepper

For the chilli jam

75ml/5 tbsp olive oil
4 large onions, diced
4 garlic cloves, chopped
1–2 green chillies, seeded and sliced
30ml/2 tbsp dark brown soft sugar

1 First make the chilli jam. Heat the oil in a frying pan until hot, then add the onions and the garlic. Reduce the heat to low, then cook for 20 minutes, stirring frequently, until the onions are very soft.

COOK'S TIP

Stored in an airtight jar in the fridge, the chilli jam will keep for up to 1 week

2 Leave the onion mixture to cool, then transfer to a food processor or blender. Add the chillies and sugar and blend until smooth, then return the mixture to the saucepan. Cook for a further 10 minutes, stirring frequently, until the liquid evaporates and the mixture has the consistency of jam. Cool slightly.

3 To make the fritters, squeeze the courgettes in a dish towel to remove any excess liquid, then combine with the Parmesan, eggs, flour and salt and pepper.

4 Heat enough oil to cover the base of a large frying pan. Add 30ml/2 tbsp of the mixture for each fritter and cook three fritters at a time. Cook for 2–3 minutes on each side until golden, then keep warm while you cook the rest of the fritters. Drain on kitchen paper and serve warm with a spoonful of the chilli jam.

Charred Artichokes with Lemon Oil Dip

Here is a lip-smacking change from traditional fare.

Serves 4

15ml/1 tbsp lemon juice or white
 wine vinegar
2 artichokes, trimmed
12 garlic cloves, unpeeled
90ml/6 tbsp olive oil
1 lemon
sea salt
flat leaf parsley sprigs, to garnish

1 Preheat the oven to 200°C/
 400°F/Gas 6. Add the lemon
juice or vinegar to a bowl of cold
water. Cut each artichoke into
wedges. Pull the hairy choke out
from the centre of each wedge and
discard, then drop the wedges into
the water.

2 Drain the wedges and place in
 a roasting tin with the garlic
and 45ml/3 tbsp of the oil. Toss
well to coat. Sprinkle with salt and
roast for 40 minutes, until tender
and a little charred.

COOK'S TIP

Artichokes are usually boiled, but
dry-heat cooking also works very
well. If you can get young
artichokes, try roasting them over
a barbecue.

---

3 Meanwhile, make the dip.
 Using a small, sharp knife
thinly pare away two strips of rind
from the lemon. Lay the strips of
rind on a board and carefully
scrape away any remaining pith.
Place the rind in a small pan with
water to cover. Bring to the boil,
then simmer for 5 minutes. Drain
the rind, refresh in cold water, then
chop coarsely. Set aside.

4 Arrange the cooked artichokes
 on a serving plate and leave to
cool for 5 minutes. Using the back
of a fork gently flatten the garlic
cloves so that the flesh squeezes
out of the skins. Transfer the garlic
flesh to a bowl, mash to a paste,
then add the lemon rind. Squeeze
the juice from the lemon, then,
using the fork, whisk the remaining
olive oil and the lemon juice into
the garlic mixture. Garnish with
the parsley. Serve the artichokes
still warm with the lemon oil dip.

Sesame Seed-coated Falafel with Tahini dip

Sesame seeds are used to give a delightfully crunchy coating to these spicy chick-pea patties. Serve with the tahini yogurt dip, and some warmed pitta bread too if you like.

INGREDIENTS

Serves 6

250g/9oz/1⅓ cups dried chick-peas

2 garlic cloves, crushed

1 red chilli, seeded and finely sliced

5ml/1 tsp ground coriander

5ml/1 tsp ground cumin

15ml/1 tbsp chopped fresh mint

15ml/1 tbsp chopped fresh parsley

2 spring onions, finely chopped

1 large egg, beaten

sesame seeds, for coating

sunflower oil, for frying

salt and ground black pepper

For the tahini yogurt dip

30ml/2 tbsp light tahini

200g/7oz/scant 1 cup natural live yogurt

5ml/1 tsp cayenne pepper, plus extra for sprinkling

15ml/1 tbsp chopped fresh mint

1 spring onion, finely sliced

fresh herbs, to garnish

1 Place the chick-peas in a bowl, cover with cold water and leave to soak overnight. Drain and rinse the chick-peas, then place in a saucepan and cover with cold water. Bring to the boil and boil rapidly for 10 minutes. Reduce the heat; simmer for 1½–2 hours until tender.

2 Meanwhile, make the tahini yogurt dip. Mix together the tahini, yogurt, cayenne pepper and mint in a small bowl. Sprinkle the spring onion and extra cayenne pepper on top and chill in the fridge until required.

3 Combine the chick-peas with the garlic, chilli, ground spices, herbs, spring onions and seasoning, then mix in the egg. Place in a food processor and blend until the mixture forms a coarse paste. If the paste seems too soft, chill it for 30 minutes.

4 Form the chilled chick-pea paste into 12 patties with your hands, then roll each one in the sesame seeds to coat thoroughly.

5 Heat enough oil to cover the base of a large frying pan Fry the falafel, in batches if necessary, for 6 minutes, turning once. Serve with the tahini yogurt dip garnished with fresh herbs.

Deep-fried New Potatoes with Saffron Aïoli

Serve these crispy little golden potatoes dipped into a wickedly garlicky mayonnaise – then sit back and watch them disappear in a matter of minutes!

Serves 4

1 egg yolk

2.5ml/½ tsp Dijon mustard

300ml/½ pint/1¼ cups extra virgin
 olive oil

15–30ml/1–2 tbsp lemon juice

1 garlic clove, crushed

2.5ml/½ tsp saffron strands

20 baby, new or salad potatoes

vegetable oil, for deep-frying

salt and ground black pepper

1 For the saffron aïoli, put the egg yolk in a bowl with the Dijon mustard and a pinch of salt. Stir to mix together well. Beat in the olive oil very slowly, drop by drop at first and then in a very thin stream. Stir in the lemon juice.

2 Season the aïoli with salt and pepper then add the crushed garlic and beat into the mixture thoroughly to combine.

3 Place the saffron in a small bowl and add 10ml/2 tsp hot water. Press the saffron with the back of a teaspoon, to extract the colour and flavour, and leave to infuse for 5 minutes. Beat the saffron and the liquid into the aïoli.

4 Cook the potatoes in their skins in boiling salted water for 5 minutes, then turn off the heat. Cover the pan and leave for 15 minutes. Drain the potatoes, then dry them thoroughly in a dish towel.

5 Heat a 1cm/½in layer of vegetable oil in a deep pan. When the oil is very hot, add the potatoes and fry quickly, turning them constantly, until crisp and golden all over. Drain on kitchen paper and serve hot with the saffron aïoli.

Leek and Onion Tartlets

Baking in individual tins makes for easier serving for a starter and it looks attractive too. You could make tiny tartlets for parties.

INGREDIENTS

Serves 6

25g/1oz/2 tbsp butter

1 onion, thinly sliced

2.5ml/½ tsp dried thyme

450g/1lb leeks, thinly sliced

50g/2oz Gruyère or Emmenthal
   cheese, grated

3 eggs

300ml/½ pint/1¼ cups single cream

pinch of freshly grated nutmeg

salt and ground black pepper

mixed salad leaves, to serve

For the pastry

175g/6oz/1⅓ cup plain flour

75g/3oz/6 tbsp cold butter

1 egg yolk

30–45ml/2–3 tbsp cold water

2.5ml/½ tsp salt

1 To make the pastry, sift the flour into a bowl and add the butter. Using your fingertips, rub the butter into the flour until it resembles fine breadcrumbs. Make a well in the centre of the mixture.

2 Beat together the egg yolk, water and salt, pour into the well and combine the flour and liquid until it begins to stick together. Form into a ball. Wrap and chill for 30 minutes.

3 Butter six 10cm/4in tartlet tins. On a lightly floured surface, roll out the dough until 3mm/⅛in thick, then using a 12.5cm/5in cutter, cut as many rounds as possible. Gently ease the rounds into the tins, pressing the pastry firmly into the base and sides. Re-roll the trimmings and line the remaining tins. Prick the bases all over and chill in the fridge for 30 minutes.

4 Preheat the oven to 190°C/375°F/Gas 5. Line the pastry cases with foil and fill with baking beans. Place on a baking sheet and bake for 6–8 minutes until golden at the edges. Remove the foil and beans and bake for a further 2 minutes until the bases appear dry. Transfer to a wire rack to cool. Reduce the oven temperature to 180°C/350°F/Gas 4.

5 In a large frying pan, melt the butter over a medium heat, then add the onion and thyme and cook for 3–5 minutes until the onion is just softened, stirring frequently. Add the thinly sliced leeks and cook for 10–12 minutes until they are soft and tender, stirring occasionally. Divide the leek mixture among the pastry cases and sprinkle each with cheese, dividing it evenly.

6 In a medium bowl, beat the eggs, cream, nutmeg and salt and pepper. Place the pastry cases on a baking sheet and pour in the egg mixture. Bake for 15–20 minutes until set and golden. Transfer the tartlets to a wire rack to cool slightly, then remove them from the tins and serve warm or at room temperature with salad leaves.

Chive Scrambled Eggs in Brioches

This is an indulgent, truly delicious and slightly quirky start to a meal – quick and easy too.

INGREDIENTS

Serves 4

115g/4oz/½ cup unsalted butter

75g/3oz/generous 1 cup brown cap
   mushrooms, finely sliced

4 individual brioches

8 eggs

15ml/1 tbsp snipped fresh chives, plus
   extra to garnish

salt and ground black pepper

1 Preheat the oven to 180°C/
350°F/Gas 4. Place a quarter of
the butter in a frying pan and heat
until melted. Fry the mushrooms
for about 3 minutes or until soft,
then set aside and keep warm.

2 Slice the tops off the brioches,
then scoop out the centres and
discard. Put the brioches and lids
on a baking sheet and bake for
5 minutes until they are hot and
slightly crisp.

3 Meanwhile, beat the eggs
lightly and season to taste.
Heat the remaining butter in a
heavy-based saucepan over a
gentle heat. When the butter has
melted and is foaming slightly, add
the eggs. Using a wooden spoon,
stir constantly to ensure the egg
does not stick.

4 Continue to stir gently until
about three-quarters of the egg
is semi-solid and creamy – this
should take 2–3 minutes. Remove
the pan from the heat – the egg
will continue to cook in the heat
from the pan – then stir in the
snipped chives.

5 To serve, spoon a little of the
mushrooms into the base of
each brioche and top with the
scrambled eggs. Sprinkle with
extra chives, balance the brioche
lids on top and serve immediately.

COOK'S TIP

Timing and temperature are
crucial for perfect scrambled
eggs. When cooked for too long
over too high a heat, eggs become
dry and crumbly; if they are
undercooked they will be sloppy
and unappealing.

Risotto Frittata

Half omelette, half risotto, this makes a delightful and satisfying starter. If possible, cook each frittata separately, and preferably in a small, cast-iron pan, so that the eggs cook quickly underneath but stay moist on top. Or cook in one large pan and serve in wedges.

INGREDIENTS

Serves 4

30–45ml/2–3 tbsp olive oil

1 small onion, finely chopped

1 garlic clove, crushed

1 large red pepper, seeded and cut into thin strips

150g/5oz/¾ cup risotto rice

400–475ml/14–16fl oz/1⅔–2 cups simmering vegetable stock

25–40g/1–1½ oz/2–3 tbsp butter

175g/6oz/2½ cups button mushrooms, finely sliced

60ml/4 tbsp freshly grated Parmesan cheese

6–8 eggs

salt and ground black pepper

1 Heat 15ml/1 tbsp oil in a large frying pan and fry the onion and garlic over a gentle heat for 2–3 minutes until the onion begins to soften but does not brown. Add the pepper and cook, stirring, for 4–5 minutes, until soft.

2 Stir in the rice and cook gently for 2–3 minutes, stirring all the time, until the grains are evenly coated with oil.

3 Add a quarter of the vegetable stock and season with salt and pepper. Stir over a low heat until the stock has been absorbed. Continue to add more stock, a little at a time, allowing the rice to absorb the liquid before adding more. Continue cooking in this way until the rice is *al dente*.

4 In a separate small pan, heat a little of the remaining oil and some of the butter and quickly fry the mushrooms until golden. Transfer to a plate.

5 When the rice is tender, remove from the heat and stir in the cooked mushrooms and the Parmesan cheese.

6 Beat together the eggs with 40ml/8 tsp cold water and season well. Heat the remaining oil and butter in an omelette pan and add the risotto mixture. Spread the mixture out in the pan, then immediately add the beaten egg, tilting the pan so that the omelette cooks evenly. Fry over a moderately high heat for 1–2 minutes, then transfer to a warmed plate and serve.

COOK'S TIP

Don't be impatient while cooking the rice. Adding the stock gradually ensures a wonderfully creamy consistency.

Pears and Stilton

Stilton is the classic British blue cheese, but you could use blue Cheshire instead, or even a non-British cheese such as Gorgonzola.

Serves 4

4 ripe pears, lightly chilled

75g/3oz blue Stilton

50g/2oz curd cheese

ground black pepper

watercress sprigs, to garnish

For the dressing

45ml/3 tbsp light olive oil

15ml/1 tbsp lemon juice

10ml/2 tsp toasted poppy seeds

salt and ground black pepper

2 Cut the pears in half lengthways, then scoop out the cores and cut away the calyx from the rounded end.

3 Beat together the Stilton, curd cheese and a little pepper. Divide this mixture among the cavities in the pears.

4 Shake the dressing to mix it again, then spoon it over the pears. Serve garnished with some watercress sprigs.

1 First make the dressing, place the olive oil and lemon juice, poppy seeds and seasoning in a screw-top jar and then shake together until emulsified.

COOK'S TIP

Comice pears are a good choice for this dish, being very juicy and aromatic. For a dramatic colour contrast, select the excellent sweet and juicy Red Williams.

Vegetable Tempura

Tempura is a Japanese type of savoury fritter. Originally prawns were used, but vegetables can be cooked in the egg batter successfully too. The secret of making the incredibly light batter is to use really cold water, and to have the oil at the right temperature before you start cooking the fritters.

INGREDIENTS

Serves 4

2 courgettes
½ aubergine
1 large carrot
½ small Spanish onion
1 egg
120ml/4fl oz/½ cup iced water
115g/4oz/1 cup plain flour
salt and ground black pepper
vegetable oil, for deep-frying
sea salt flakes, lemon slices and Japanese
   soy sauce (*shoyu*), to serve

1 Using a potato peeler, pare strips of peel from the courgettes and aubergine to give a striped effect.

2 Using a chef's knife, cut the courgettes, aubergine and carrot into strips measuring about 7.5–10cm/3–4in long and 3mm/⅛in wide. Place in a colander and sprinkle with salt. Put a small plate over and weight it down. Leave for 30 minutes, then rinse. Drain then dry with kitchen paper.

3 Thinly slice the onion from top to base, discarding the plump pieces in the middle. Separate the layers so that there are lots of fine, long strips. Mix all the vegetables together and season with salt and pepper.

4 Make the batter immediately before frying. Mix the egg and iced water in a bowl, then sift in the flour. Mix briefly with a fork or chopsticks. Do not overmix: the batter should remain lumpy. Add the vegetables to the batter and mix to combine.

5 Half-fill a wok with oil and heat to 180ºC/350ºF. Scoop up a heaped tablespoonful of the mixture at a time and carefully lower it into the oil. Deep-fry in batches for about 3 minutes, until golden brown and crisp. Drain on kitchen paper.

6 Serve each portion with salt, slices of lemon and a tiny bowl of Japanese soy sauce for dipping.

> ### COOK'S TIP
>
> Other suitable vegetables for tempura include mushrooms and slices of red, green, yellow or orange peppers.

Tortilla Wrap with Tabbouleh & Avocado

To be successful, tabbouleh needs spring onions, lemon juice, plenty of fresh herbs and lots of freshly ground black pepper. It is best served at room temperature and goes very well with the chilli and avocado mixture.

INGREDIENTS

Serves 6

175g/6oz/1 cup bulgur wheat
30ml/2 tbsp chopped fresh mint
30ml/2 tbsp chopped fresh flat
  leaf parsley
1 bunch spring onions (about 6), sliced
½ cucumber, diced
50ml/2fl oz/¼ cup extra virgin olive oil
juice of 1 large lemon
salt and freshly ground black pepper
1 ripe avocado, stoned, peeled and diced
juice of ½ lemon
½ red chilli, seeded and sliced
1 garlic clove, crushed
½ red pepper, seeded and finely diced
4 wheat tortillas, to serve
flat leaf parsley, to garnish (optional)

1 To make the tabbouleh, place the bulgur wheat in a large heatproof bowl and pour over enough boiling water to cover. Leave for 30 minutes until the grains are tender but still retain a little resistance to the bite. Drain thoroughly in a sieve, then tip back into the bowl.

2 Add the mint, parsley, spring onions and cucumber to the bulgur wheat and mix thoroughly. Blend together the olive oil and lemon juice and pour over the tabbouleh, season to taste and toss well to mix. Chill for 30 minutes to allow the flavours to mingle.

3 To make the avocado mixture, place the avocado in a bowl and add the lemon juice, chilli and garlic. Season to taste and mash with a fork to form a smooth purée. Stir in the red pepper.

4 Warm the tortillas in a dry frying pan and serve either flat, folded or rolled up with the tabbouleh and avocado mixture. Garnish with parsley, if using.

COOK'S TIP

The soaking time for bulgur wheat can vary. For the best results, follow the instructions on the packet and taste the grain every now and again to check whether it is tender enough.

Indian Mee Goreng

This colourful noodle dish is truly international, combining Indian, Chinese and Western ingredients. In Singapore and Malaysia can be bought in many streets from one of the numerous hawkers' stalls.

INGREDIENTS

Serves 6

450g/1lb fresh yellow egg noodles
60-90ml/ 4–6 tbsp vegetable oil
115g/4oz fried beancurd (tofu)
2 eggs
30ml/2tbsp water
1 onion sliced
1 garlic clove, crushed
15ml/1tbsp light soy sauce
30-45ml/2–3tbsp tomato ketchup
15ml/1 tbsp chilli sauce (or to taste)
1 large cooked potato, diced
4 spring onions, shredded
1–2 fresh green chillies, seeded and finely
    sliced (optional)

1 Bring a large saucepan of water to the boil, add the fresh egg noodles and cook for just 2 minutes. Drain the noodles and immediately rinse them under cold water to stop them cooking. Drain again and set aside.

2 If using fried beancurd, cut each cube in half, refresh it in a pan of boiling water, then drain well Heat 30/2 tbsp of the oil in a large frying pan If using using plain beancurd, cut into cubes and fry until brown, then lift it out with a slotted spoon and set aside.

3 Beat the eggs with the water and seasoning. Add to the oil in the frying pan and cook without stirring until set. Flip over, cook the other side , then slide it out of the pan, roll up and slice thinly.

4 Heat the remaining oil in a wok and fry the onion and garlic for 2-3 minutes. Ad the drained noodles, soy sauce, ketchup and chilli sauce. Toss well over medium heat for 2 minutes, then add the diced potato. Reserve a few spring onions for garnish and stir the rest into the noodles with the chilli, if using, and the beancurd.

5 When hot , stir in the omelette. Serve on a hot platter garnished with the remaining spring onions.

Twice-baked Gruyère and Potato Soufflé

A great starter dish, this recipe can be prepared in advance if you are entertaining and given its second baking just before you serve it up.

INGREDIENTS

Serves 4

225g/8oz floury potatoes
2 eggs, separated
175g/6oz/1½ cups Gruyère, grated
50g/2oz/½ cup self-raising flour
50g/2oz spinach leaves
butter, for greasing
salt and ground black pepper
salad leaves, to serve

3 Finely chop the spinach and fold into the potato mixture.

4 Whip the egg whites until they form soft peaks. Fold a little of the egg white into the mixture to slacken it slightly. Using a large spoon, fold the remaining egg white into the mixture.

5 Grease 4 large ramekin dishes. Pour the mixture into the dishes; place on a baking sheet. Bake for 20 minutes. Remove from the oven and allow to cool.

6 Turn the soufflés out on to a baking sheet and scatter with the remaining cheese. Bake again for 5 minutes; serve with salad leaves.

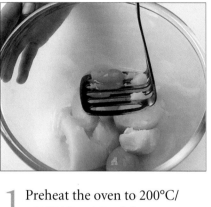

1 Preheat the oven to 200°C/ 400°F/Gas 6. Peel the potatoes and cook in lightly salted boiling water for 20 minutes until very tender. Drain and mash with the egg yolks.

2 Stir in half of the Gruyère cheese and all of the flour. Season to taste with salt and ground black pepper.

VARIATION
~

For a different flavouring try replacing the Gruyère with a crumbled blue cheese, such as Stilton or Shropshire Blue, which have a stronger taste.

Fried Rice Balls Stuffed with Mozzarella

These deep-fried balls of risotto go by the name of Suppli al Telefono in their native Italy. Stuffed with mozzarella cheese, they are very popular snacks, which is hardly surprising as they are quite delicious. They make a wonderful start to any meal.

INGREDIENTS

Serves 4

1 quantity Risotto alla Milanese, made without the saffron and with vegetable stock (see page 126)

3 eggs

breadcrumbs and plain flour, to coat

115g/4oz/⅔ cup mozzarella cheese, cut into small cubes

oil, for deep-frying

dressed curly endive and cherry tomatoes, to serve

1 Put the risotto in a bowl and allow it to cool completely. Beat two of the eggs, and stir them into the cooled risotto until well mixed.

2 Use your hands to form the rice mixture into balls the size of a large egg. If the mixture is too moist to hold its shape well, stir in a few spoonfuls of breadcrumbs. Poke a hole in the centre of each ball with your finger, then fill it with small cubes of mozzarella, and close the hole over again with the rice mixture.

3 Heat the oil for deep-frying until a small piece of bread sizzles as soon as it is dropped in.

4 Spread some flour on a plate. Beat the remaining egg in a shallow bowl. Sprinkle another plate with breadcrumbs. Roll the balls in the flour, then in the egg, and finally in the breadcrumbs.

5 Fry the rice balls, a few at a time, in the hot oil until golden and crisp. Drain on kitchen paper while the remaining balls are being fried and keep warm. Serve at once, with a simple salad of dressed curly endive leaves and cherry tomatoes.

COOK'S TIP

These provide the perfect solution as to what to do with leftover risotto, as they are best made with a cold mixture, cooked the day before.

Mini Baked Potatoes with Blue Cheese

These miniature potatoes can be eaten with the fingers. They provide a great way of starting off an informal supper party.

INGREDIENTS

Makes 20

20 small new or salad potatoes

60ml/4 tbsp vegetable oil

coarse salt

120ml/4fl oz/½ cup soured cream

25g/1oz blue cheese, crumbled

30ml/2 tbsp snipped fresh chives, to garnish

1 Preheat the oven to 180°C/ 350°F/Gas 4. Wash and dry the potatoes. Toss with the oil in a bowl to coat.

2 Dip the potatoes in the coarse salt to coat lightly. Spread the potatoes out on a baking sheet. Bake for 45–50 minutes until the potatoes are tender.

3 In a small bowl, combine the soured cream and blue cheese, mixing together well.

COOK'S TIP

This dish works just as well as a light snack; if you don't want to be bothered with lots of fiddly small potatoes, simply bake an ordinary baking potato.

4 Cut a cross in the top of each potato. Press gently with your fingers to open the potatoes.

5 Top each potato with a dollop of the blue cheese mixture. Place on a serving dish and garnish with the chives. Serve hot or at room temperature.

Buckwheat Blinis with Mushroom Caviar

These little Russian pancakes are traditionally served with fish roe caviar and soured cream. Here is a vegetarian alternative that uses a selection of delicious wild mushrooms in place of the fish roe. The blinis can be made ahead of time and warmed in the oven before topping.

INGREDIENTS

Serves 4

115g/4oz/1 cup strong white bread flour

50g/2oz/½ cup buckwheat flour

2.5ml/½ tsp salt

300ml/½ pint/1¼ cups milk

5ml/1 tsp dried yeast

2 eggs, separated

200ml/7fl oz/scant 1 cup soured cream or crème fraîche

For the caviar

350g/12oz mixed wild mushrooms such as field mushrooms, orange birch bolete, bay boletus, oyster and St George's mushrooms

5ml/1 tsp celery salt

30ml/2 tbsp walnut oil

15ml/1 tbsp lemon juice

45ml/3 tbsp chopped fresh parsley

ground black pepper

1 To make the caviar, trim and chop the mushrooms, then place them in a glass bowl, toss with the celery salt and cover with a weighted plate.

2 Leave the mushrooms for 2 hours until the juices have run out into the base of the bowl. Rinse the mushrooms thoroughly to remove the salt, drain and press out as much liquid as you can with the back of a spoon. Return them to the bowl and toss with walnut oil, lemon juice, parsley and a twist of pepper. Chill in the fridge until ready to serve.

3 Sift the two flours together with the salt in a large mixing bowl. Gently warm the milk to approximately blood temperature. Add the yeast, stirring until dissolved, then pour into the flour, add the egg yolks and stir to make a smooth batter. Cover with a clean damp dish towel and leave in a warm place for 1 hour.

4 Whisk the egg whites in a clean grease-free bowl until stiff then fold into the risen batter.

5 Heat an iron pan or griddle to a moderate temperature. Moisten with oil, then drop spoonfuls of the batter on to the surface. When bubbles rise to the top, turn them over and cook briefly on the other side. Spoon on the soured cream orcrème fraîche, top with the mushroom caviar and serve.

FAMILY
FAVOURITES

Eggs Benedict

There is still debate over who created this recipe but the most likely story credits a Mr and Mrs LeGrand Benedict, regulars at New York's Delmonico's restaurant, who complained there was nothing new on the lunch menu. This dish was created as a result.

INGREDIENTS

Serves 4

5ml/1 tsp vinegar

4 eggs

2 English muffins or 4 rounds of bread

butter, for spreading

4 thick slices cooked ham, trimmed to fit the muffins

fresh chives, to garnish

For the sauce

3 egg yolks

30ml/2 tbsp fresh lemon juice

1.5ml/¼ tsp salt

115g/4oz/½ cup butter

30ml/2 tbsp single cream

ground black pepper

1 To make the sauce, blend the egg yolks, lemon juice, and salt in a food processor or blender for 15 seconds.

2 Melt the butter in a small saucepan until it bubbles (do not let it brown). With the motor running, pour the hot butter into the food processor through the feed tube in a slow, steady stream. Turn off the machine as soon as all the butter has been added.

3 Scrape the sauce into the top of a double boiler, over just simmering water. Stir for 2–3 minutes, until thickened. (If it curdles, whisk in 15ml/1 tbsp boiling water.) Stir in the cream and season with pepper. Keep warm over the hot water.

4 Bring a shallow pan of water to the boil. Stir in the vinegar. Break each egg into a cup or jug, then slide it carefully into the water. Carefully and gently turn the white around the yolk with a slotted spoon. Cook until the egg is set to your taste, about 3–4 minutes. Remove from the pan and place on kitchen paper to drain. Very gently cut any ragged edges off the eggs with a small knife or scissors.

5 While the eggs are poaching, split and toast the muffins or toast the bread slices. Butter while they are still warm.

6 Place a piece of ham, which you may brown in butter if you wish, on each muffin half or slice of toast. Place an egg on each ham-topped muffin. Spoon the warm sauce over the eggs, garnish with chives and serve.

COOK'S TIP

For a special treat grate a little white or black truffle on top before serving.

Three-colour Fish Kebabs

Don't leave the fish to marinate for more than an hour. The lemon juice will start to break down the fibres of the fish after this time and it will then be difficult to avoid overcooking it.

INGREDIENTS

Serves 4

120ml/4fl oz/½ cup olive oil

finely grated rind and juice of
   1 large lemon

5ml/1 tsp crushed chilli flakes

350g/12oz monkfish fillet, cubed

350g/12oz swordfish fillet, cubed

350g/12oz thick salmon fillet or
   steak, cubed

2 red, yellow or orange peppers, cored,
   seeded and cut into squares

30ml/2 tbsp finely chopped fresh flat
   leaf parsley

salt and ground black pepper

For the sweet tomato and chilli salsa

225g/8oz ripe tomatoes, finely chopped

1 garlic clove, crushed

1 fresh red chilli, seeded and chopped

45ml/3 tbsp extra virgin olive oil

15ml/1 tbsp lemon juice

15ml/1 tbsp finely chopped fresh flat
   leaf parsley

pinch of sugar

1 Put the oil in a shallow glass or china bowl and add the lemon rind and juice, the chilli flakes and pepper to taste. Whisk to combine, then add the fish chunks. Turn to coat evenly.

2 Add the pepper squares, stir, then cover and marinate in a cool place for 1 hour, turning occasionally with a slotted spoon.

3 Thread the fish and peppers on to eight oiled metal skewers, reserving the marinade. Barbecue or grill the skewered fish for 5–8 minutes, turning once.

4 Meanwhile, make the salsa by mixing all the ingredients in a bowl, and seasoning to taste with salt and pepper. Heat the reserved marinade in a small pan, remove from the heat and stir in the parsley, with salt and pepper to taste. Serve the kebabs hot, with the marinade spooned over, accompanied by the salsa.

COOK'S TIP

Use tuna instead of swordfish, if you like. It has a similar meaty texture and will be equally successful.

Risotto Alla Milanese

This classic risotto is often served with the hearty beef stew, osso buco, but it also makes a delicious first course in its own right.

INGREDIENTS

Serves 5–6

about 1.2 litres/2 pints/5 cups beef or
   chicken stock
good pinch of saffron strands
75g/3oz/6 tbsp butter
1 onion, finely chopped
275g/10oz/1½ cups risotto rice
75g/3oz/1 cup freshly grated
   Parmesan cheese
salt and ground black pepper

1 Bring the stock to the boil, then reduce to a low simmer. Ladle a little stock into a small bowl. Add the saffron strands and leave to infuse.

2 Melt 50g/2oz/4 tbsp of the butter in a large saucepan until foaming. Add the onion and cook gently for about 3 minutes, stirring frequently, until softened but not browned at all.

3 Add the rice. Stir until the grains start to swell and burst, then add a few ladlefuls of the stock, with the saffron liquid and salt and pepper to taste. Stir over a low heat until the stock has been absorbed. Add the remaining stock, a few ladlefuls at a time, allowing the rice to absorb all the liquid before adding more, and stirring constantly. After about 20–25 minutes, the rice should be just tender and the risotto golden yellow, moist and creamy.

4 Gently stir in about two-thirds of the grated Parmesan and the remaining butter. Heat through until the butter has melted, then taste for seasoning. Transfer the risotto to a warmed serving bowl or platter and serve hot, with the remaining grated Parmesan served separately.

Hard-boiled Eggs with Tuna Sauce

The combination of eggs with a tasty tuna mayonnaise makes a nourishing first course that is quick and easy to prepare.

INGREDIENTS

Serves 6

6 extra large eggs

200g/7oz can tuna in olive oil

3 anchovy fillets

15ml/1 tbsp capers, drained

lemon juice

30ml/2 tbsp olive oil

salt and ground black pepper

drained capers and anchovy fillets, to
garnish (optional)

For the mayonnaise

1 egg yolk, at room temperature

5ml/1 tsp Dijon mustard

5ml/1 tsp white wine vinegar or
lemon juice

150ml/¼ pint/⅔ cup olive oil

1 Boil the extra large eggs for
12–14 minutes. Drain under
cold water. Peel carefully and
set aside.

2 Make the mayonnaise by
whisking the egg yolk, mustard
and white wine vinegar or lemon
juice together in a small bowl.
Whisk in the oil a few drops at a
time until 45–60ml/3–4 tbsp oil
have been incorporated. Pour in
the remaining oil in a slow stream,
whisking constantly.

3 Place the tuna with its oil, the
anchovies, capers, lemon juice
and olive oil in a blender or a food
processor. Process until smooth.

4 Fold the tuna sauce into the
mayonnaise. Season with black
pepper, and extra salt if necessary.
Chill for at least 1 hour.

5 To serve, cut the eggs in half
lengthways. Arrange them on
a serving platter. Spoon over the
sauce, and garnish with capers and
anchovy fillets, if using. Serve the
eggs chilled.

Spinach Empanadillas

These are little pastry turnovers, filled with ingredients that have a strong Moorish influence – pine nuts and raisins. Serve with pre-dinner drinks at an informal supper party, allowing two to three per person.

INGREDIENTS

Makes 20

25g/1oz/2 tbsp raisins

25ml/1½ tbsp olive oil

450g/1lb fresh spinach, washed and chopped

6 drained canned anchovies, chopped

2 garlic cloves, finely chopped

25g/1oz/⅓ cup pine nuts, chopped

1 egg, beaten

350g/12oz puff pastry

salt and ground black pepper

1 To make the filling, soak the raisins in a little warm water for 10 minutes. Drain, then chop roughly. Heat the oil in a large sauté pan or wok, add the spinach, stir, then cover and cook over a low heat for about 2 minutes. Uncover, turn up the heat and let any liquid evaporate. Add the anchovies, garlic and seasoning, then cook, stirring, for a further minute. Remove from the heat, add the raisins and pine nuts, and cool.

2 Preheat the oven to 180°C/ 350°F/Gas 4. Roll out the pastry to a 3mm/⅛in thickness.

3 Using a 7.5cm/3in pastry cutter, cut out 20 rounds, re-rolling the dough if necessary. Place about two teaspoonfuls of the filling in the middle of each round, then brush the edges with a little water. Bring up the sides of the pastry and seal well.

4 Press the edges of the pastry together with the back of a fork. Brush with beaten egg. Place the turnovers on a lightly greased baking sheet and bake for about 15 minutes, until golden. Serve the empanadillas warm.

Thai-style Seafood Pasties

*These elegant appetizer-size pasties
are filled with fish, prawns and Thai
fragrant rice, and are subtly
flavoured with fresh coriander,
garlic and ginger.*

INGREDIENTS

Makes 18

plain flour, for dusting

500g/1¼lb puff pastry, thawed if frozen

1 egg, beaten with 30ml/2 tbsp water

lime twists, to garnish

For the filling

275g/10oz skinned white fish fillets,
    such as cod or haddock

seasoned plain flour

8–10 large raw prawns

15ml/1 tbsp sunflower oil

about 75g/3oz/6 tbsp butter

6 spring onions, finely sliced

1 garlic clove, crushed

225g/8oz/2 cups cooked Thai fragrant rice

4cm/1½ in piece fresh root
    ginger, grated

10ml/2 tsp finely chopped fresh coriander

5ml/1 tsp finely grated lime rind

1 Preheat the oven to 190°C/
375°F/Gas 5. Make the filling.
Cut the fish into 2cm/¾in cubes
and dust with seasoned flour. Peel
and devein the prawns and cut
each one into four pieces.

2 Heat half of the oil and
15g/½oz/1 tbsp of the butter
in a frying pan. Fry the spring
onions gently for 2 minutes.

3 Add the garlic and fry for a
further 5 minutes, until the
onions are very soft. Transfer to a
large bowl.

4 Heat the remaining oil and a
further 25g/1oz/2 tbsp of the
butter in a clean pan. Fry the fish
pieces briefly. As soon as they
begin to turn opaque, use a slotted
spoon to transfer them to the bowl
with the spring onions. Cook the
prawns in the fat remaining in the
pan. When they begin to change
colour, lift them out and add them
to the bowl.

5 Add the cooked rice to the
bowl, with the fresh root
ginger, coriander and grated lime
rind. Mix, taking care not to break
up the fish.

6 Dust the work surface with a
little flour. Roll out the pastry
and cut into 10cm/4in rounds.
Place spoonfuls of filling just off
centre on the pastry rounds. Dot
with a little of the remaining
butter. Dampen the edges of the
pastry with a little of the egg wash,
fold one side of the pastry over
the filling and press the edges
together firmly.

7 Place the pasties on two lightly
greased baking sheets.
Decorate them with the pastry
trimmings, if you like, and brush
them with egg wash. Bake in the
oven for 12–15 minutes or until
golden brown all over.

8 Transfer to a plate and garnish
with lime twists.

Fish Sausages

This recipe originated in Hungary during the seventeenth century. It is still popular today..

INGREDIENTS

Serves 4

375g/13oz fish fillets, such as perch, pike, carp or cod, skinned

1 white bread roll

75ml/5 tbsp milk

25ml/1½ tbsp chopped fresh flat leaf parsley

2 eggs, well beaten

50g/2oz/½ cup plain flour

50g/2oz/1 cup fine fresh white breadcrumbs

oil, for shallow frying

salt and ground black pepper

deep-fried parsley sprigs and lemon wedges, dusted with paprika, to garnish

1 Mince or process the fish coarsely in a food processor or blender. Soak the roll in the milk for about 10 minutes, then squeeze it out. Mix the fish and bread together before adding the chopped parsley, one of the eggs and plenty of seasoning.

2 Using your fingers, shape the fish mixture into 10cm/4in long sausages, making them about 2.5cm/1 in thick.

3 Carefully roll the fish "sausages" in the flour, then in the remaining egg and finally in the breadcrumbs.

4 Heat the oil in a pan then slowly cook the "sausages" until golden brown all over. (You may need to work in batches.) Drain well on crumpled kitchen paper. Garnish with the deep-fried parsley sprigs and lemon wedges dusted with paprika.

Deep-fried Whitebait

*A spicy coating on these fish gives
this favourite dish a crunchy bite.*

INGREDIENTS

Serves 6

115g/4oz/1 cup plain flour

2.5ml/½ tsp curry powder

2.5ml/½ tsp ground ginger

2.5ml/½ tsp ground cayenne pepper

pinch of salt

1.2kg/2½ lb whitebait, thawed if frozen

vegetable oil, for deep-frying

lemon wedges, to garnish

1 Mix together the plain flour,
curry powder, ground ginger,
cayenne pepper and a little salt in a
large bowl.

2 Coat the fish in the seasoned
flour, covering them evenly.

3 Heat the oil in a large, heavy-
based saucepan until it reaches
a temperature of 190°C/375°F. Fry
the whitebait in batches for about
2–3 minutes until the fish is golden
and crispy.

4 Drain the whitebait well on
kitchen paper. Keep warm in
a low oven until you have cooked
all the fish. Serve at once
garnished with lemon wedges for
squeezing over.

Paella Croquettes

Paella is probably Spain's most famous dish, and here it is used for a tasty fried tapas. In this recipe, the paella is cooked from scratch, but you could, of course, use leftover paella instead.

INGREDIENTS

Serves 4

pinch of saffron threads

150ml/¼ pint/⅔ cup white wine

30ml/2 tbsp olive oil

1 small onion, finely chopped

1 garlic clove, finely chopped

150g/5oz/⅔ cup risotto rice

300ml/½ pint/1¼ cups hot chicken stock

50g/2oz /½ cup cooked prawns, peeled, deveined and coarsely chopped

50g/2oz cooked chicken, coarsely chopped

75g/3oz/⅔ cup petits pois, thawed if frozen

30ml/2 tbsp freshly grated Parmesan cheese

1 egg, beaten

30ml/2 tbsp milk

75g/3oz/1½ cups fresh white breadcrumbs

vegetable or olive oil, for shallow-frying

salt and ground black pepper

flat leaf parsley, to garnish

1 Stir the saffron into the wine in a small bowl; set aside.

2 Heat the oil in a saucepan and gently fry the onion and garlic for 5 minutes until softened. Stir in the risotto rice and cook, stirring, for 1 minute.

3 Keeping the heat fairly high, add the wine and saffron mixture to the pan, stirring until it is all absorbed. Gradually add the stock, stirring until all the liquid has been absorbed and the rice is cooked – this should take about 20 minutes.

4 Stir in the prawns, chicken, petits pois and freshly grated Parmesan. Season to taste. Leave to cool slightly, then use two tablespoons to shape the mixture into 16 small lozenges.

5 Mix the egg and milk in a shallow bowl. Spread out the breadcrumbs on a sheet of foil. Dip the croquettes in the egg mixture, then coat them evenly in the breadcrumbs.

6 Heat the oil in a large frying pan. Then shallow fry the croquettes for 4–5 minutes until crisp and golden brown. Work in batches. Drain on kitchen paper and keep hot. Serve garnished with a sprig of flat leaf parsley.

Herby Plaice Fritters

Serve these baby croquettes with a tartare sauce if you like. Simply chop some capers and gherkins, and stir into home-made or good quality shop-bought mayonnaise. Season to taste.

Serves 4

450g/1lb plaice fillets

300ml/½ pint/1¼ cups milk

450g/1lb cooked potatoes

1 fennel bulb, finely chopped

45ml/ 3 tbsp chopped fresh parsley

2 eggs

15g/½ oz/1 tbsp unsalted butter

250g/9oz/2 cups white breadcrumbs

25g/1oz/2 tbsp sesame seeds

oil, for deep-frying

salt and ground black pepper

1 Gently poach the plaice fillets in the milk for approximately 15 minutes until the fish flakes. Drain and reserve the milk.

2 Peel the skin off the fish and remove any bones. In a food processor fitted with a metal blade, process the fish, potatoes, fennel, parsley, eggs and butter.

3 Add 30ml/2 tbsp of the reserved cooking milk and season with salt and plenty of ground black pepper. Mix well. Chill for 30 minutes then shape into twenty even-size croquettes with your hands.

4 Mix together the breadcrumbs and sesame seeds, then roll the croquettes in this mixture to form a good coating. Heat the oil in a large, heavy-based saucepan until it is hot enough to brown a cube of stale bread in 30 seconds. Deep-fry the croquettes in small batches for about 4 minutes until they are golden brown all over. Drain well on kitchen paper and serve the fritters hot.

Thai Fish Cakes with Cucumber Relish

These wonderful small fish cakes are a very familiar and popular starter. They are usually accompanied with Thai beer or choose a robust oaked Chardonnay instead.

INGREDIENTS

Makes about 12

300g/11oz white fish fillet, such as cod, cut into chunks
30ml/2 tbsp red curry paste
1 egg
30ml/2 tbsp fish sauce
5ml/1 tsp granulated sugar
30ml/2 tbsp cornflour
3 kaffir lime leaves, shredded
15ml/1 tbsp chopped fresh coriander
50g/2oz green beans, finely sliced
oil, for frying
Chinese mustard cress, to garnish

For the cucumber relish
60ml/4 tbsp Thai coconut or rice vinegar
60ml/4 tbsp water
50g/2oz sugar
1 whole bulb pickled garlic
1 cucumber, quartered and sliced
4 shallots, finely sliced
15ml/1 tbsp chopped fresh root ginger

1 To make the cucumber relish, bring the vinegar, water and sugar to the boil. Stir until the sugar dissolves, then remove from the heat and leave to cool.

2 Combine the rest of the relish ingredients together in a bowl and pour the vinegar mixture over.

3 Combine the fish, curry paste and egg in a food processor and process well. Transfer the mixture to a bowl, add the rest of the ingredients, except the oil and garnish, and mix well.

4 Mould and shape the mixture into cakes about 5cm/2in in diameter and 5mm/¼in thick.

5 Heat the oil in a wok or deep-fat fryer. Fry the fish cakes, working in small batches, for about 4–5 minutes or until golden brown. Remove and drain on kitchen paper. Keep warm in a low oven. Garnish with Chinese mustard cress and serve with a little cucumber relish spooned on the side.

Crab and Ricotta Tartlets

Use the meat from a freshly cooked crab, weighing about 450g/1lb, if you can. Otherwise, look out for frozen brown and white crabmeat.

INGREDIENTS

Serves 4

225g/8oz/2 cups plain flour

pinch of salt

115g/4oz/½ cup butter, diced

225g/8oz/1 cup ricotta

15ml/1 tbsp grated onion

30ml/2 tbsp freshly grated
   Parmesan cheese

2.5ml/½ tsp mustard powder

2 eggs, plus 1 egg yolk

225g/8oz crabmeat

30ml/2 tbsp chopped fresh parsley

2.5–5ml/½–1 tsp anchovy essence

5–10ml/1–2 tsp lemon juice

salt and cayenne pepper

salad leaves, to garnish

1 Preheat the oven to 200°C/400°F/Gas 6. Sift the flour and salt into a bowl, add the butter and rub it in until the mixture resembles fine bread-crumbs. Stir in about 60ml/4 tbsp cold water to make a firm dough.

2 Turn the dough on to a floured surface and knead lightly. Roll out the pastry and use to line four 10cm/4in tartlet tins. Prick the bases with a fork, then chill for 30 minutes.

3 Line the pastry cases with grease-proof paper and fill with baking beans. Bake for 10 minutes, then remove the paper and beans. Return to the oven and bake for a further 10 minutes.

4 Place the ricotta, grated onion, Parmesan and mustard powder in a bowl and beat until soft. Gradually beat in the eggs and egg yolk.

5 Gently stir in the crabmeat and chopped parsley, then add the anchovy essence, lemon juice, salt and cayenne pepper, to taste.

6 Remove the tartlet cases from the oven and reduce the temperature to 180°C/350°F/Gas 4. Spoon the filling into the cases and bake for 20 minutes, until set and golden brown. Serve hot with a garnish of salad leaves.

Grilled King Prawns with Romesco Sauce

This sauce, originally from the Catalan region of Spain, is served with fish and seafood. Its main ingredients are sweet pepper, tomatoes, garlic and almonds.

Serves 6–8

24 raw king prawns

30–45ml/2–3 tbsp olive oil

flat leaf parsley, to garnish

lemon wedges, to serve

For the sauce

2 well-flavoured tomatoes

60ml/4 tbsp olive oil

1 onion, chopped

4 garlic cloves, chopped

1 canned pimiento, chopped

2.5ml/½ tsp dried chilli flakes or powder

75ml/5 tbsp fish stock

30ml/2 tbsp white wine

10 blanched almonds

15ml/1 tbsp red wine vinegar

salt, to taste

3 Toast the almonds under the grill until golden. Transfer to a blender or food processor and grind coarsely. Add the remaining 30ml/2 tbsp of oil, the vinegar and the last garlic clove and process until evenly combined. Add the tomato and pimiento sauce and process until smooth. Season with salt, to taste.

4 Remove the heads from the prawns leaving them otherwise unpeeled and, with a sharp knife, slit each one down the back and remove the dark vein. Rinse and pat dry on kitchen paper. Preheat the grill. Toss the prawns in olive oil, then spread out in the grill pan. Grill for about 2–3 minutes on each side, until pink. Arrange on a serving platter with the lemon wedges, and the sauce in a small bowl. Serve at once, garnished with parsley.

1 To make the sauce, immerse the tomatoes in boiling water for about 30 seconds, then refresh them under cold water. Peel away the skins and roughly chop the tomato flesh.

2 Heat 30ml/2 tbsp of the oil in a pan, add the onion and 3 of the garlic cloves and cook until soft. Add the pimiento, tomatoes, chilli, fish stock and wine, then cover and simmer for 30 minutes.

Breaded Sole Batons

Goujons of lemon sole are coated in seasoned flour and then in breadcrumbs, and fried until deliciously crispy. They are served with piquant tartare sauce.

INGREDIENTS

Serves 4

275g/10oz lemon sole fillets, skinned

2 eggs

115g/4oz/1½ cups fine fresh breadcrumbs

75g/3oz/6 tbsp plain flour

salt and ground black pepper

vegetable oil, for frying

tartare sauce and lemon wedges, to serve

1 Cut the fish fillets into long diagonal strips about 2cm/¾in wide, using a sharp knife.

2 Break the eggs into a shallow dish and beat well with a fork. Place the breadcrumbs in another shallow dish. Put the flour in a large polythene bag and season with salt and plenty of ground black pepper.

3 Dip the fish strips in the egg, turning to coat well. Place on a plate and then taking a few at a time, shake them in the bag of flour. Dip the fish strips in the egg again, then in the breadcrumbs, turning to coat well. Place on a tray in a single layer, not touching. Let the coating set for at least 10 minutes.

4 Heat 1cm/½in oil in a large frying pan over a medium-high heat. When the oil is hot (a cube of bread will sizzle) try the fish strips for about 2–2½ minutes in batches, turning once, taking care not to overcrowd the pan. Drain on kitchen paper and keep warm. Serve the fish with tartare sauce and lemon wedges.

Kansas City Fritters

These fritters are made wonderfully light by the egg whites which are whisked separately before being folded in.

INGREDIENTS

Makes 8

210g/7½oz/1¼ cups canned
   sweetcorn, drained
2 eggs, separated
40g/1½oz/⅓ cup flour
90ml/6 tbsp milk
1 small courgette, grated
2 bacon rashers, diced
2 spring onions, finely chopped
good pinch of cayenne pepper
45ml/3 tbsp sunflower oil
salt and ground black pepper
coriander sprigs, to garnish

For the salsa

3 tomatoes, peeled, seeded and diced
½ small red pepper, seeded and diced
½ small onion, diced
15ml/1 tbsp lemon juice
15ml/1 tbsp chopped fresh coriander
dash of Tabasco sauce

3 Stir in the grated courgette, bacon, spring onions, cayenne pepper and seasoning and set aside until required.

4 Place the egg whites in a clean bowl and whisk until stiff. Gently fold into the corn batter mixture with a metal spoon.

5 Heat 30ml/2 tbsp of the oil in a large frying pan and place four large spoonfuls of the mixture into the oil. Fry over a moderate heat for 2–3 minutes on each side until golden, then drain on kitchen paper. Keep warm in the oven while frying the remaining four fritters, adding the rest of the oil if necessary.

6 Serve two fritters each, garnished with coriander sprigs and a spoonful of the chilled tomato salsa.

1 To make the salsa, place all the ingredients in a bowl, mix well and season. Cover and chill.

2 Empty the corn into a large bowl and mix in the egg yolks. Add the flour and blend in with a wooden spoon. When the mixture begins to thicken, gradually blend in the milk.

Chicken Croquettes

This recipe comes from Rebato's, a tapas bar in London. The chef there makes croquettes with a number of different flavourings; this version uses chicken.

INGREDIENTS

Serves 4

25g/1oz/2 tbsp butter
25g/1oz/¼ cup plain flour
150ml/¼ pint/⅔ cup milk
15ml/1 tbsp olive oil
1 boneless chicken breast with skin, about 3oz, diced
1 garlic clove, finely chopped
1 small egg, beaten
50g/2oz/1 cup fresh white breadcrumbs
vegetable oil, for deep-frying
salt and ground black pepper
flat leaf parsley, to garnish
lemon wedges, to serve

1 Melt the butter in a small saucepan. Add the flour and cook gently, stirring, for 1 minute. Gradually beat in the milk to make a smooth, very thick sauce. Cover with a lid and remove from the pan from the heat.

2 Heat the oil in a frying pan and cook the chicken with the garlic for 5 minutes, until the chicken is lightly browned and cooked through.

3 Turn the contents of the frying pan into a food processor or blender and process until finely chopped. Stir the chicken into the sauce, mixing it well. Add plenty of salt and pepper to taste. Leave to cool completely.

4 Shape into eight even-size sausages, then dip each in egg and then breadcrumbs. Deep-fry in hot oil for 4 minutes until crisp and golden. Drain on kitchen paper and serve garnished with parsley and lemon wedges for squeezing.

Chicken Bitki

This is a popular Polish dish and makes an attractive starter when offset by deep red beetroot and vibrant green salad leaves.

INGREDIENTS

Makes 12

15g/½oz/1 tbsp butter, melted

115g/4oz flat mushrooms, finely chopped

50g/2oz/1 cup fresh white breadcrumbs

350g/12oz chicken breasts or guinea fowl, minced or finely chopped

2 eggs, separated

1.5ml/¼ tsp grated nutmeg

30ml/2 tbsp plain flour

45ml/3 tbsp oil

salt and ground black pepper

salad leaves and grated pickled beetroot, to serve

1 Melt the butter in a pan and fry the mushrooms for about 5 minutes until soft and the juices have evaporated. Allow to cool.

2 Mix the mushrooms and the breadcrumbs, the chicken or guinea fowl, egg yolks, nutmeg, salt and pepper together.

3 Whisk the egg whites until stiff. Stir half into the chicken mixture to slacken it, then fold in the remainder.

4 Shape into 12 even-size meatballs, about 7.5cm/3in long and 2.5cm/1in wide. Roll in the flour to coat.

5 Heat the oil in a frying pan and fry the bitki for about 10 minutes, turning until evenly golden brown and cooked through. Serve hot with salad leaves and pickled beetroot.

Chicken Parcels

These home-made chicken parcels look splendid piled high and golden brown.

Makes 35

225g/8oz/2 cups strong white flour,
   plus extra for dusting
2.5ml/½ tsp salt
2.5ml/½ tsp caster sugar
5ml/1 tsp easy-blend dried yeast
25g/1oz/2 tbsp butter, softened
1 egg, beaten, plus a little extra
90ml/6 tbsp warm milk
lemon wedges, to serve

For the filling
1 small onion, finely chopped
175g/6oz/1½ cups minced chicken
15ml/1 tbsp sunflower oil
75ml/5 tbsp chicken stock
30ml/2 tbsp chopped fresh parsley
pinch of grated nutmeg
salt and ground black pepper

1 Sift the flour, salt and sugar into a large bowl. Stir in the dried yeast, then make a well in the centre of the flour.

2 Add the butter, egg and milk and mix to a soft dough. Turn on to a lightly floured surface and knead for 10 minutes, until the dough is smooth and elastic.

3 Put the dough in a clean bowl, cover with clear film and then leave in a warm place to rise for 1 hour, or until the dough has doubled in size.

4 Meanwhile, fry the onion and chicken in the oil for about 10 minutes. Add the stock and simmer for 5 minutes. Stir in the parsley, grated nutmeg and salt and ground black pepper. Then leave to cool.

5 Preheat the oven to 220°C/ 425°F/Gas 7. Knead the dough, then roll it out until it is 3mm/⅛in thick. Stamp out rounds with a 7.5cm/3in cutter.

6 Brush the edges with beaten egg. Put a little filling in the middle, then press the edges together. Leave to rise on oiled baking sheets, covered with oiled clear film, for 15 minutes. Brush with a little more egg. Bake for 5 minutes, then for 10 minutes at 190°C/375°F/Gas 5, until well risen. Serve with lemon wedges.

Stuffed Garlic Mushrooms with Prosciutto

Field mushrooms can vary greatly in size. Choose similar-size specimens with undamaged edges.

INGREDIENTS

Serves 4

1 onion, chopped

75g/3oz/6 tbsp unsalted butter

8 field mushrooms

15g/½oz/¼ cup dried ceps, bay boletus or saffron milk-caps, soaked in warm water for 20 minutes

1 garlic clove, crushed

75g/3oz/¾ cup fresh breadcrumbs

1 egg

75ml/5 tbsp chopped fresh parsley

15ml/1 tbsp chopped fresh thyme

salt and ground black pepper

115g/4oz prosciutto di Parma or San Daniele, thinly sliced

fresh parsley, to garnish

1 Preheat the oven to 190°C/ 375°F/Gas 5. Fry the onion gently in half the butter for 6–8 minutes until soft but not coloured. Meanwhile, break off the stems of the field mushrooms, setting the caps aside. Drain the dried mushrooms and chop these and the stems of the field mushrooms finely. Add to the onion together with the garlic and cook for a further 2–3 minutes.

2 Transfer the mixture to a bowl, add the breadcrumbs, egg, herbs and seasoning. Melt the remaining butter in a small pan and generously brush over the mushroom caps. Arrange the mushrooms on a baking sheet and spoon in the filling. Bake in the oven for 20–25 minutes until they are well browned.

3 Top each mushroom with a slice of prosciutto, garnish with parsley and serve.

COOK'S TIP

• Garlic mushrooms can be easily prepared in advance ready to go into the oven.

• Fresh breadcrumbs can be made and then frozen. They can be taken from the freezer as they are required and do not need to be defrosted first.

Barbecue-Glazed Chicken Skewers

Known as Yakitori in Japan, these skewers are popular throughout the country and are often served as an appetizer with drinks.

INGREDIENTS

Makes 12 skewers and 8 wing pieces

8 chicken wings

4 chicken thighs, skinned

4 spring onions, blanched and cut into
    short lengths

For the basting sauce

60ml/4 tbsp sake

75ml/5 tbsp/⅓ cup dark soy sauce

30ml/2 tbsp tamari sauce

15ml/1 tbsp mirin, or sweet sherry

15ml/1 tbsp sugar

1 Remove the wing tip of the chicken at the first joint. Chop through the second joint, revealing the two narrow bones. Take hold of the bones with a clean cloth and pull, turning the meat around the bones inside out. Remove the smaller bone and discard. Set the wings aside.

2 Bone the chicken thighs and cut the meat into large dice. Thread the spring onions and thigh meat on to 12 skewers.

3 Measure the basting sauce ingredients into a stainless-steel or enamel saucepan and simmer until reduced by two-thirds. Cool.

4 Heat the grill to a moderately high temperature. Grill the skewers without applying any oil. When juices begin to emerge from the chicken baste liberally with the sauce. Allow a further 3 minutes for the chicken on skewers and not more than 5 minutes for the wings.

Pork Satay

Originating in Indonesia, satay are skewers of meat marinated with spices and grilled quickly over charcoal. It's street food at its best, prepared by vendors with portable grills who set up stalls at every road side and market place. It makes a great-tasting starter too. It's not too filling and it's bursting with flavour. You can make satay with chicken, beef or lamb. Serve with satay sauce, and a cucumber relish if you like.

INGREDIENTS

Makes about 20

450g/1lb lean pork
5ml/1 tsp grated fresh root ginger
1 lemon grass stalk, finely chopped
3 garlic cloves, finely chopped
15ml/1 tbsp medium curry paste
5ml/1 tsp ground cumin
5ml/1 tsp ground turmeric
60ml/4 tbsp coconut cream
30ml/2 tbsp fish sauce
5ml/1 tsp granulated sugar
oil, for brushing
fresh herbs, to garnish

For the satay sauce
250ml/8fl oz/1 cup coconut milk
30ml/2 tbsp red curry paste
75g/3oz crunchy peanut butter
120ml/4fl oz/½ cup chicken stock
45ml/3 tbsp brown sugar
30ml/2 tbsp tamarind juice
15ml/1 tbsp fish sauce
2.5ml/½ tsp salt

1 Cut the pork thinly into 5cm/2in strips. Mix together the fresh root ginger, lemon grass, garlic, curry paste, cumin, turmeric, coconut cream, fish sauce and sugar.

2 Pour over the pork and leave to marinate for about 2 hours.

3 Meanwhile, make the sauce. Heat the coconut milk over a medium heat, then add the red curry paste, peanut butter, chicken stock and sugar.

4 Cook and stir until smooth, about 5–6 minutes. Add the tamarind juice, fish sauce and salt to taste.

5 Thread the meat on to skewers. Brush with oil and grill over charcoal or under a preheated grill for 3–4 minutes on each side, turning occasionally, until cooked and golden brown. Serve with the satay sauce garnished with fresh herbs.

Spicy Koftas

These koftas will need to be cooked in batches. Keep them hot when they are cooked while you cook the rest.

INGREDIENTS

Makes 20–25

450g/1lb lean minced beef or lamb

30ml/2 tbsp finely ground ginger

30ml/2 tbsp finely minced garlic

4 green chillies, finely chopped

1 small onion, finely chopped

1 egg

2.5ml/½ tsp turmeric

5ml/1 tsp garam masala

50g/2oz coriander leaves, chopped

4–6 mint leaves, chopped, or 2.5ml/½ tsp mint sauce

175g/6oz raw potato

salt, to taste

vegetable oil, for deep-frying

1 Place the beef or lamb in a large bowl along with the ginger, garlic, chillies, onion, egg, spices and herbs. Grate the potato into the bowl, and season with salt. Knead together to blend well and form a soft dough.

COOK'S TIP

Leftover koftas can be coarsely chopped and packed into pitta bread spread with chutney or relish for a quick and delicious snack.

2 Using your fingers, shape the kofta mixture into portions the size of golf balls. You should be able to make 20 to 25 koftas. Leave the balls to rest at room temperature for about 25 minutes.

3 In a wok or frying pan, heat the oil to medium-hot and fry the koftas in small batches until they are golden brown in colour. Drain well and serve hot.

Golden Parmesan Chicken

Served cold with the garlicky mayonnaise these morsels of chicken make a great appetizer, especially if served informally as finger food.

INGREDIENTS

Serves 4

4 chicken breast fillets, skinned

75g/3oz/1½ cups fresh white
   breadcrumbs

40g/1½ oz Parmesan cheese, finely grated

30ml/2 tbsp chopped fresh parsley

2 eggs, beaten

120ml/4fl oz/½ cup good-quality
   mayonnaise

120ml/4fl oz/½ cup fromage frais

1–2 garlic cloves, crushed

50g/2oz/4 tbsp butter, melted

salt and ground black pepper

1 Cut each fillet into four or five chunks. Mix together the breadcrumbs, Parmesan, parsley and seasoning in a shallow dish.

2 Dip the chicken pieces in the egg, then into the breadcrumb mixture. Place in a single layer on a baking sheet; chill for 30 minutes.

3 Meanwhile, to make the garlic mayonnaise, mix together the mayonnaise, fromage frais and garlic, and season to taste with ground black pepper. Spoon the mayonnaise into a small serving bowl. Chill until required.

4 Preheat the oven to 180°C/ 350°F/Gas 4. Drizzle the melted butter over the chicken pieces and cook them for about 20 minutes, until crisp and golden. Serve the chicken immediately accompanied by the garlic mayonnaise for dipping.

Savoury Pork Pies

These little pies come from Spain and are fun to eat.

INGREDIENTS

Makes 12 pastries

350g/12oz shortcrust pastry, thawed
    if frozen

For the filling
15ml/1 tbsp vegetable oil
1 onion, chopped
1 clove garlic, crushed
5ml/1 tsp thyme
115g/4oz/1 cup minced pork
5ml/1 tsp paprika
1 hard-boiled egg, chopped
1 gherkin, chopped
30ml/2 tbsp chopped
    fresh parsley
vegetable oil, for deep-frying
salt and ground black pepper

1 To make the filling, heat the vegetable oil in a saucepan or wok and soften the onion, garlic and thyme without browning, for about 3–4 minutes. Add the pork and paprika then brown evenly for 6–8 minutes. Season well, turn out into a bowl and cool. When the mixture is cool, add the hard-boiled egg, gherkin and parsley.

2 Turn the pastry out on to a floured work surface and roll out to a 38cm/15in square. Cut out 12 circles 13cm/5in in diameter. Place 15ml/1 tbsp of the filling on each circle, moisten the edges with a little water, fold over and seal.

3 Heat the vegetable oil in a deep-fryer fitted with a basket, to 196°C/385°F. Place three pies at a time in the basket and deep-fry until golden brown. Frying should take at least 1 minute or the inside filling will not be heated through. Serve warm in a basket covered with a napkin.

Deep-fried Lamb Patties

These patties are a tasty North African speciality – called kibbeh – of minced meat and bulgur wheat. They are sometimes stuffed with additional meat and deep fried. Moderately spiced, they're good served with yogurt.

INGREDIENTS

Serves 6

450g/1lb lean lamb (or lean minced lamb or beef)
salt and ground black pepper
oil, for deep-frying
avocado slices and coriander sprigs, to serve

For the patties
225g/8oz/1⅓ cups bulgur wheat
1 red chilli, seeded and roughly chopped
1 onion, roughly chopped

For the stuffing
1 onion, finely chopped
50g/2oz/⅔ cup pine nuts
30ml/2 tbsp olive oil
7.5ml/1½ tsp ground allspice
60ml/4 tbsp chopped fresh coriander

1 If necessary, roughly cut up the lamb and process the pieces in a blender or food processor until minced. Divide the minced meat into two equal portions.

2 For the patties, soak the bulgur wheat for 15 minutes in cold water. Drain then process in a blender or a food processor with the chilli, onion, half the meat and salt and pepper.

3 For the stuffing, fry the onion and pine nuts in the oil for 5 minutes. Add the allspice and remaining minced meat and fry gently, breaking up the meat with a wooden spoon, until browned. Stir in the coriander and seasoning.

4 Turn the patty mixture out on to a work surface and shape into a cake. Cut into 12 wedges.

5 Flatten one piece and spoon some stuffing into the centre. Bring the edges of the patty up over the stuffing, ensuring that the filling is completely encased.

6 Heat oil to a depth of 5cm/2in in a large pan until a few patty crumbs sizzle on the surface.

7 Lower half of the filled patties into the oil and fry for about 5 minutes until golden. Drain on kitchen paper and keep hot while cooking the remainder. Serve with avocado slices and coriander sprigs.

Chicken with Lemon and Garlic

Extremely easy to cook and delicious to eat, serve this succulent tapas dish with home-made aioli if you like.

INGREDIENTS

Serves 4

225g/8oz skinless chicken breast fillets

30ml/2 tbsp olive oil

1 shallot, finely chopped

4 garlic cloves, finely chopped

5ml/1tsp paprika

juice of 1 lemon

30ml/2 tbsp chopped fresh parsley

salt and ground black pepper

flat leaf parsley, to garnish

lemon wedges, to serve

1 Sandwich the chicken breast fillets between two sheets of clear film or greaseproof paper. Bat out with a rolling pin or meat mallet until the fillets are about 5mm/¼ in thick.

2 Cut the chicken into strips about 1cm/½ in wide. Heat the oil in a large frying pan. Stir-fry the chicken strips with the shallot, garlic and paprika over a high heat for about 3 minutes until lightly browned and cooked through. Add the lemon juice and parsley with salt and pepper to taste. Serve with lemon wedges, garnished with flat leaf parsley.

STARTERS FOR
SPECIAL
OCCASIONS

Asparagus with Raspberry Dressing

Asparagus and raspberries complement each other. The sauce gives this starter a real zing.

INGREDIENTS

Serves 4

675g/1½lb thin asparagus spears
30ml/2 tbsp raspberry vinegar
2.5ml/½ tsp salt
5ml/1 tsp Dijon mustard
25ml/1½ tbsp sunflower oil
30ml/2 tbsp soured cream or
    natural yogurt
ground white pepper
175g/6oz/1 cup fresh raspberries

1 Fill a large wide frying pan or wok with water 10cm/4in deep and bring to the boil.

2 Trim the tough ends of the asparagus spears. If desired, remove the "scales" using a vegetable peeler.

3 Tie the asparagus spears into two bundles. Lower the bundles into the boiling water and cook until just tender, about 2 minutes.

4 Using a fish slice, carefully remove the asparagus bundles from the frying pan or wok and immerse in cold water to stop the cooking. Drain then untie the bundles. Pat dry with kitchen paper. Chill the asparagus in the fridge for at least 1 hour.

5 Combine the vinegar and salt in a bowl and stir with a fork until dissolved. Stir in the mustard. Gradually stir in the oil until it is blended. Add the soured cream or yogurt and pepper to taste.

6 To serve, place the asparagus on individual plates and drizzle the dressing across the middle of the spears. Garnish with the fresh raspberries.

Wild Mushroom and Fontina Tarts

Italian fontina cheese gives these tarts a creamy, nutty flavour. Serve them warm with rocket leaves.

INGREDIENTS

Serves 4

25g/1oz/½ cup dried wild mushrooms

30ml/2 tbsp olive oil

1 red onion, chopped

2 garlic cloves, chopped

30ml/2 tbsp medium-dry sherry

1 egg

120ml/4fl oz/½ cup single cream

25g/1oz fontina cheese, thinly sliced

salt and ground black pepper

rocket leaves, to serve

For the pastry

115g/4oz/1 cup wholemeal flour

50g/2oz/4 tbsp unsalted butter

25g/1oz/¼ cup walnuts, roasted
   and ground

1 egg, lightly beaten

1 To make the pastry, rub the flour and butter together until the mixture resembles fine breadcrumbs. Add the nuts then the egg; mix to a soft dough. Wrap, then chill for 30 minutes.

2 Meanwhile, soak the dried wild mushrooms in 300ml/ ½ pint/1¼ cups boiling water for 30 minutes. Drain and reserve the liquid. Fry the onion in the oil for 5 minutes, then add the garlic and fry for about 2 minutes, stirring.

3 Add the soaked mushrooms and cook for 7 minutes over a high heat until the edges become crisp. Add the sherry and the reserved liquid. Cook over a high heat for about 10 minutes until the liquid evaporates. Season and set aside to cool.

COOK'S TIP
~

You can prepare the pastry cases in advance, bake them blind for 10 minutes, then store in an airtight container for up to 2 days.

---

4 Preheat the oven to 200°C/400°F/Gas 6. Lightly grease four 10cm/4in tart tins. Roll out the pastry on a lightly floured work surface and use to line the tart tins.

5 Prick the pastry, line with greaseproof paper and baking beans and bake blind for about 10 minutes. Remove the paper and the beans.

6 Whisk the egg and cream to mix, add to the mushroom mixture, then season to taste. Spoon into the pastry cases, top with cheese slices and bake for 18 minutes until the filling is set. Serve warm with rocket.

Tomato and Courgette Timbales

Timbales are baked savoury custards typical of the South of France, and mainly made with light vegetables. This combination is delicious as a starter. It can be served warm or cool. Try other combinations if you like and choose different herbs as well.

INGREDIENTS

Serves 4

a little butter

2 courgettes, about 175g/6oz

2 firm, ripe vine tomatoes, sliced

2 eggs plus 2 egg yolks

45ml/3 tbsp double cream

15ml/1 tbsp fresh tomato sauce or passata

10ml/2 tsp chopped fresh basil or oregano
   or 5ml/1 tsp dried

salt and ground black pepper

salad leaves, to serve

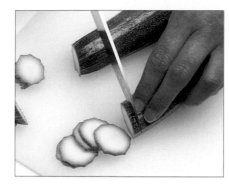

1 Preheat the oven to 180°C/ 350°F/Gas 4. Lightly butter four large ramekins. Top and tail the courgettes then cut them into thin slices. Put them into a steamer and steam over boiling water for 4–5 minutes. Drain well in a colander then layer the courgettes in the ramekins alternating with the sliced tomatoes.

2 Whisk together the eggs, cream, tomato sauce or passata, herbs and seasoning. Pour the egg mixture into the ramekins. Place them in a roasting tin and half fill with hot water. Bake the ramekins for 20–30 minutes until the custard is just firm.

3 Cool slightly then run a knife round the rims and carefully turn out on to small plates. Serve with salad leaves.

COOK'S TIP

Don't overcook the timbales or the texture of the savoury custard will become rubbery.

Risotto with Four Cheeses

This is a very rich dish. Serve it for a special dinner-party first course, with a light, dry sparkling white wine to accompany it.

INGREDIENTS

Serves 4–6

40g/1½oz/3 tbsp butter

1 small onion, finely chopped

1.2 litres/2 pints/5 cups chicken stock, preferably home-made

350g/12oz/1¾ cups risotto rice

200ml/7fl oz/scant 1 cup dry white wine

50g/2oz/½ cup grated Gruyère cheese

50g/2oz/½ cup diced taleggio cheese

50g/2oz/½ cup diced Gorgonzola cheese

50g/2oz/⅔ cup freshly grated Parmesan cheese

salt and ground black pepper

chopped fresh flat leaf parsley, to garnish

1 Melt the butter in a large, heavy-based saucepan or deep frying pan and fry the onion over a gentle heat for about 4–5 minutes, stirring frequently, until softened and lightly browned. Pour the stock into a separate pan and heat it to simmering point.

2 Add the rice to the onion mixture, stir until the grains start to swell and burst, then add the wine. Stir until it stops sizzling and most of it has been absorbed by the rice, then pour in a little of the hot stock. Add salt and ground black pepper to taste. Stir the rice over a low heat until the stock has been absorbed.

3 Gradually add the remaining stock, a little at a time, allowing the rice to absorb the liquid before adding more, and stirring constantly. After about 20–25 minutes the rice will be *al dente* and the risotto will have a creamy consistency.

4 Turn off the heat under the pan, then add the Gruyère, taleggio, the Gorgonzola and 30ml/2 tbsp of the Parmesan. Stir gently until the cheeses have melted, then taste for seasoning. Spoon into a serving bowl and garnish with parsley. Serve the remaining Parmesan separately.

Vegetable Tarte Tatin

This upside-down tart combines Mediterranean vegetables with rice, garlic, onions and olives.

INGREDIENTS

Serves 4

30ml/2 tbsp sunflower oil

about 25ml/1½ tbsp olive oil

1 aubergine, sliced lengthways

1 large red pepper, seeded and cut into
   long strips

5 tomatoes

2 red shallots, finely chopped

1–2 garlic cloves, crushed

150ml/¼ pint/⅔ cup white wine

10ml/2 tsp chopped fresh basil

225g/8oz/2 cups cooked white or brown
   long grain rice

40g/1½oz/⅔ cup stoned black
   olives, chopped

350g/12oz puff pastry, thawed if frozen

ground black pepper

salad leaves, to serve

1 Preheat the oven to 190°C/
375°F/Gas 5. Heat the
sunflower oil with 15ml/1 tbsp of
the olive oil and fry the aubergine
slices for 4–5 minutes on each side.
Drain on kitchen paper.

COOK'S TIP
~

Courgettes and mushrooms could
be used as well, or instead of, the
aubergines and peppers, or use
strips of lightly browned chicken.

---

2 Add the pepper strips to the oil
remaining in the pan, turning
them to coat. Cover the pan with a
lid or foil and sweat the peppers
over a moderately high heat for
5–6 minutes, stirring occasionally,
until the pepper strips are soft and
flecked with brown.

3 Slice two of the tomatoes and
set them aside. Plunge the
remaining tomatoes briefly into
boiling water, then peel them, cut
them into quarters and remove the
core and seeds. Chop the tomato
flesh roughly.

4 Heat the remaining oil in the
frying pan and fry the shallots
and garlic for 3–4 minutes until
softened. Then add the chopped
tomatoes and cook for a few
minutes until softened. Stir in the
wine and basil, with black pepper
to taste. Bring to the boil, then
remove from the heat and stir in
the cooked rice and black olives.

5 Arrange the tomato slices,
aubergine slices and peppers
in a single layer on the base of a
heavy, 30cm/12in, shallow
ovenproof dish. Spread the rice
mixture on top.

6 Roll out the pastry to a circle
slightly larger than the
diameter of the dish and place on
top of the rice, tucking the overlap
down inside the dish.

7 Bake for 25–30 minutes, until
the pastry is golden and risen.
Cool slightly, then invert the tart
on to a large, warmed serving
plate. Serve in slices, with some
salad leaves.

Black Pasta with Ricotta

This is designer pasta – which is coloured with squid ink – at its most dramatic, the kind of dish you are most likely to see at a fashionable Italian restaurant. Serve it for a smart dinner-party first course – it will create a great talking point.

INGREDIENTS

Serves 4

300g/11oz dried black pasta

60ml/4 tbsp ricotta cheese, as fresh
   as possible

60ml/4 tbsp extra virgin olive oil

1 small fresh red chilli, seeded and
   finely chopped

small handful of fresh basil leaves

salt and ground black pepper

1 Cook the black pasta in salted boiling water according to the instructions on the packet. Meanwhile, put the ricotta in a bowl, add salt and pepper to taste and use a little of the hot water from the pasta pan to mix it to a smooth, creamy consistency. Taste for seasoning.

2 Drain the pasta. Heat the oil gently in the clean pan and add the pasta with the chilli and salt and pepper to taste. Toss quickly over a high heat to combine.

3 Divide the pasta equally among four warmed bowls, then top with the ricotta cheese. Sprinkle with the basil leaves and serve immediately. Each diner tosses their own portion of pasta and cheese.

> ### COOK'S TIP
> ❧
> If you prefer, use green spinach-flavoured pasta or red tomato-flavoured pasta in place of the black pasta.

Paglia e Fieno with Walnuts and Gorgonzola

Cheese and nuts are popular ingredients for pasta sauces. The combination is very rich, so reserve this dish for a dinner-party starter. The contrasting colours make this dish look particularly attractive. It needs no accompaniment other than wine – a dry white would be good.

INGREDIENTS

Serves 4

275g/10oz dried paglia e fieno

25g/1oz/2 tbsp butter

5ml/1 tsp finely chopped fresh sage, or
   2.5ml/½ tsp dried, plus fresh sage
   leaves, to garnish (optional)

115g/4oz/1 cup Gorgonzola cheese, diced

45ml/3 tbsp mascarpone cheese

75ml/5 tbsp milk

50g/2oz/½ cup walnut halves, ground

30ml/2 tbsp freshly grated
   Parmesan cheese

ground black pepper

1 Cook the pasta in a large saucepan of salted boiling water, according to the instructions on the packet. Meanwhile, melt the butter in a large skillet or saucepan over a low heat, add the sage and stir it around. Sprinkle in the diced Gorgonzola and then add the mascarpone. Stir the ingredients with a wooden spoon until the cheeses start to melt. Pour in the milk and keep stirring.

2 Sprinkle in the walnuts and grated Parmesan and add plenty of black pepper. Continue to stir over a low heat until the mixture forms a creamy sauce. Do not allow it to boil or the nuts will taste bitter, and do not cook the sauce for longer than a few minutes or the nuts will begin to discolour it.

3 Drain the pasta, tip it into a warmed bowl, then add the sauce and toss well. Serve immediately, with more black pepper ground on top. Garnish with sage leaves, if using.

Lemon, Thyme and Bean Stuffed Mushrooms

Portabello mushrooms have a rich flavour and a meaty texture that go well with this fragrant herb-and-lemon stuffing. The garlicky pine nut accompaniment is a traditional Middle Eastern dish with a smooth, creamy consistency similar to that of hummus.

INGREDIENTS

Serves 4–6

200g/7oz/1 cup dried or 400g/14oz/2 cups
    drained, canned aduki beans
45ml/3 tbsp olive oil, plus extra
    for brushing
1 onion, finely chopped
2 garlic cloves, crushed
30ml/2 tbsp fresh chopped thyme or
    5ml/1 tsp dried
8 large field mushrooms, such as
    portabello mushrooms, stalks
    finely chopped
50g/2oz/1 cup fresh wholemeal
    breadcrumbs
juice of 1 lemon
185g/6½ oz/¾ cup goat's cheese,
    crumbled
salt and ground black pepper

For the pine nut sauce
50g/2oz/½ cup pine nuts, toasted
50g/2oz/1 cup cubed white bread
2 garlic cloves, chopped
200ml/7fl oz/scant 1 cup milk
45ml/3 tbsp olive oil
15ml/1 tbsp chopped fresh parsley, to
    garnish (optional)

1 If using dried beans, soak them overnight, then drain and rinse well. Place in a saucepan, add enough water to cover and bring to the boil. Boil rapidly for 10 minutes, then reduce the heat, cook for 30 minutes until tender, then drain. If using canned beans, rinse, drain well, then set aside.

2 Preheat the oven to 200°C/ 400°F/Gas 6. Heat the oil in a large heavy-based frying pan, add the onion and garlic and sauté for 5 minutes until softened. Add the thyme and the mushroom stalks and cook for a further 3 minutes, stirring occasionally, until tender.

3 Stir in the beans, breadcrumbs and lemon juice, season well, then cook for 2 minutes until heated through. Mash two-thirds of the beans with a fork or potato masher, leaving the remaining beans whole.

4 Brush a baking dish and the base and sides of the mushrooms with oil, then top each one with a spoonful of the bean mixture. Place the mushrooms in the dish, cover with foil and bake for 20 minutes. Remove the foil. Top each mushroom with some of the goat's cheese and bake for a further 15 minutes, or until the cheese is melted and bubbly and the mushrooms are tender.

5 To make the pine nut sauce, place all the ingredients in a food processor or blender and blend until smooth and creamy. Add more milk if the mixture appears too thick. Sprinkle with parsley, if using, and serve with the stuffed mushrooms.

Aubergine and Smoked Mozzarella Rolls

Slices of grilled aubergine are stuffed with smoked mozzarella, tomato and fresh basil to make an attractive hors-d'oeuvre. The rolls are also good barbecued.

INGREDIENTS

Serves 4

1 large aubergine

45ml/3 tbsp olive oil, plus extra for
    drizzling (optional)

165g/5½ oz smoked mozzarella cheese,
    cut into 8 slices

2 plum tomatoes, each cut into
    4 even-size slices

8 large basil leaves

balsamic vinegar, for drizzling (optional)

salt and ground black pepper

1 Cut the aubergine lengthways into 10 thin slices and discard the two outermost slices. Sprinkle the slices with salt and set them aside for 20 minutes. Rinse, then pat dry with kitchen paper.

2 Preheat the grill and line the rack with foil. Place the dried aubergine slices on the grill rack and brush liberally with oil. Grill for 8–10 minutes until tender and golden, turning once.

3 Remove the aubergine slices from the grill, then place a slice of mozzarella and tomato and a basil leaf in the centre of each aubergine slice, and season to taste. Fold the aubergine over the filling and cook seam-side down under the grill until heated through and the mozzarella begins to melt. Serve drizzled with olive oil and a little balsamic vinegar, if using.

Smoked Salmon and Rice Salad Parcels

Feta, cucumber and tomatoes give a Greek flavour to the salad in these parcels, a combination which goes well with the rice, especially if a little wild rice is added.

INGREDIENTS

Serves 4

175g/6oz/scant 1 cup mixed wild rice and basmati rice

8 slices smoked salmon, total weight about 350g/12oz

10cm/4in piece of cucumber, finely diced

about 225g/8oz feta cheese, cubed

8 cherry tomatoes, quartered

30ml/2 tbsp mayonnaise

10ml/2 tsp fresh lime juice

15ml/1 tbsp chopped fresh chervil

salt and ground black pepper

lime slices and fresh chervil, to garnish

1 Cook the rice according to the instructions on the packet. Drain, tip into a bowl and leave to cool completely.

2 Line four ramekins with clear film, then line each ramekin with two slices of smoked salmon, allowing the ends to overlap the edges of the dishes.

> ### COOK'S TIP
> Use smoked trout in place of the salmon if you wish.

3 Add the cucumber, feta and tomatoes to the rice, and stir in the mayonnaise, lime juice and chervil. Mix together well. Season with salt and ground black pepper to taste.

4 Spoon the rice mixture into the salmon-lined ramekins. (Any leftover mixture can be used to make a rice salad.) Then fold over the overlapping ends of salmon so that the rice mixture is completely encased.

5 Chill the parcels in the fridge for 30–60 minutes, then invert each parcel on to a plate, using the clear film to ease them out of the ramekins. Carefully peel off the clear film, then garnish each parcel with slices of lime and a sprig of fresh chervil and serve.

Quail's Eggs in Aspic with Parma Ham

These clever looking eggs in jelly are so easy to make, and are great for summer eating. Serve them with salad leaves and some home-made mayonnaise on the side.

INGREDIENTS

Makes 12

22g packet aspic powder

45ml/3 tbsp dry sherry

12 quail's eggs

6 slices of Parma ham

12 fresh coriander or flat leaf
   parsley leaves

salad leaves, to serve

1 Make up the aspic following the packet instructions but replace 45ml/3 tbsp water with the dry sherry, giving a greater depth of flavour. Leave the aspic in the fridge until it begins to thicken, but not too thick.

2 Put the quail's eggs in a pan of cold water and bring to the boil. Boil for 1½ minutes only, then pour off the hot water and leave in cold water until cold. This way the yolks should still be a little soft but the whites will be firm enough to peel when really cold.

3 Rinse 12 dariole moulds so they are damp and place them on a tray. Cut the Parma ham into 12 pieces, then roll or fold so they will fit into the moulds.

4 Place a herb leaf in the base of each mould, then put a peeled egg on top. As the jelly begins to thicken pour in enough to nearly cover each egg, holding it steady. Then put the slice of ham on the egg and pour in the rest of the jelly to fill the mould, so that when you turn them out the eggs will be sitting on the ham.

5 Transfer the tray of moulds to a cold place and then leave for 3–4 hours until set and cold. When ready to serve run a knife around the top rim of the jelly to loosen. Dip the moulds into warm, not hot, water and shake or tap gently until they appear loose. Invert on to small plates and serve with salad leaves.

Seafood Pancakes

The combination of fresh and smoked haddock imparts a wonderful flavour to the filling.

INGREDIENTS

Serves 6

For the pancakes

115g/4oz/1 cup plain flour
pinch of salt
1 egg plus 1 egg yolk
300ml/½ pint/1¼ cups milk
15ml/1 tbsp melted butter, plus extra
   for cooking
50–75g/2–3oz Gruyère cheese, grated
frisée lettuce, to serve

For the filling

225g/8oz smoked haddock fillet
225g/8oz fresh haddock fillet
300ml/½ pint/1¼ cups milk
150ml/¼ pint/⅔ cup single cream
40g/1½ oz/3 tbsp butter
40g/1½ oz/¼ cup plain flour
freshly grated nutmeg
2 hard-boiled eggs, peeled and chopped
salt and ground black pepper

1 To make the pancakes, sift the flour and salt into a bowl. Make a well in the centre and add the egg and extra yolk. Whisk the egg, starting to incorporate some of the flour.

2 Gradually add the milk, whisking all the time until the batter is smooth and has the consistency of thin cream. Stir in the measured melted butter.

3 Heat a small crêpe pan or omelette pan until hot, then rub round the inside of the pan with a pad of kitchen paper dipped in melted butter.

4 Pour about 30ml/2 tbsp of the batter into the pan, then tip the pan to coat the base evenly. Cook for about 30 seconds until the underside of the pancake is brown.

5 Flip the pancake over and cook on the other side until it is lightly browned. Repeat to make 12 pancakes, rubbing the pan with melted butter between each pancake. Stack the pancakes as you make them between sheets of greaseproof paper. Keep warm on a plate set over a pan of simmering water.

6 Put the haddock fillets in a large pan. Add the milk and poach for 6–8 minutes, until just tender. Lift out the fish using a slotted spoon and, when cool enough to handle, remove the skin and any bones. Reserve the milk.

7 Measure the single cream into a jug then strain enough of the milk into the jug to make the quantity up to 450ml/¾ pint/scant 2 cups in total.

8 Melt the butter in a pan, stir in the flour and cook gently for 1 minute. Gradually mix in the milk mixture, stirring continuously to make a smooth sauce. Cook for 2–3 minutes, until thickened. Season with salt, black pepper and nutmeg. Roughly flake the haddock and fold into the sauce with the eggs. Leave to cool.

9 Preheat the oven to 180°C/350°F/Gas 4. Divide the filling among the pancakes. Fold the sides of each pancake into the centre, then roll them up to enclose the filling completely.

10 Butter six individual ovenproof dishes and then arrange two filled pancakes in each, or butter one large dish for all the pancakes. Brush with melted butter and cook for 15 minutes. Sprinkle over the Gruyère and cook for a further 5 minutes, until warmed through. Serve hot with frisée lettuce leaves.

King Prawns in Sherry

This dish just couldn't be simpler. The sherry brings out the sweetness of the seafood perfectly.

INGREDIENTS

Serves 4

12 raw king prawns, peeled

30ml/2 tbsp olive oil

30ml/2 tbsp sherry

few drops of Tabasco sauce

salt and ground black pepper

1 Using a very sharp knife, make a shallow cut down the back of each prawn, then pull out and discard the dark intestinal tract.

2 Heat the oil in a frying pan and fry the prawns for about 2–3 minutes until pink. Pour over the sherry and season with Tabasco sauce and salt and pepper. Turn into a dish and serve the prawns immediately.

Sizzling Prawns

This dish works especially well with tiny prawns that can be eaten whole, but any type of unpeeled prawns will be fine. Choose a small casserole or frying pan that can be taken to the table for serving while the garlicky prawns are still sizzling and piping hot.

INGREDIENTS

Serves 4

2 garlic cloves, halved

25g/1oz/2 tbsp butter

1 small red chilli, seeded and finely sliced

115g/4oz/1 cup unpeeled cooked prawns

sea salt and coarsely ground black pepper

lime wedges, to serve

1 Rub the cut surfaces of the garlic cloves over the base and sides of a frying pan, then throw the garlic cloves away. Add the butter to the pan and melt over a fairly high heat until it just begins to turn golden brown.

2 Toss in the sliced red chilli and the prawns. Stir-fry for 1–2 minutes until heated through, then season to taste with sea salt and plenty of black pepper. Serve directly from the pan with lime wedges for squeezing over.

COOK'S TIP

Wear gloves when handling chillies, or wash your hands thoroughly afterwards, as the juices can cause severe irritation to sensitive skin, especially around the eyes, nose or mouth.

Crab Cakes with Tartare Sauce

Sweet crab meat is offset by a piquant tartare sauce.

Serves 4

675g/1½ lb fresh lump crab meat

1 egg, beaten

30ml/2 tbsp mayonnaise

15ml/1 tbsp Worcestershire sauce

15ml/1 tbsp sherry

30ml/2 tbsp minced fresh parsley

15ml/1 tbsp minced fresh chives or dill

salt and ground black pepper

45ml/3 tbsp olive oil

salad leaves, chives and lemon, to garnish

For the sauce

1 egg yolk

15ml/1 tbsp white wine vinegar

30ml/2 tbsp Dijon-style mustard

250ml/8fl oz/1 cup vegetable or
    groundnut oil

3ml/2 tbsp fresh lemon juice

60ml/4 tbsp minced spring onions

30ml/2 tbsp chopped drained capers

60ml/4 tbsp minced sour dill pickles

60ml/4 tbsp minced fresh parsley

1 Pick over the crab meat, removing any pieces of shell or cartilage. Keep the pieces of crab as large as possible.

2 In a mixing bowl, combine the beaten egg with the mayonnaise, Worcestershire sauce, sherry and herbs. Season with salt and lots of black pepper. Gently fold in the crab meat.

3 Divide the mixture into 8 portions and gently form each one into an oval cake. Place on a baking sheet between layers of greaseproof paper and chill for at least 1 hour.

4 Meanwhile, make the sauce. In a medium-size bowl, beat the egg yolk with a wire whisk until smooth. Add the vinegar, mustard, and salt and pepper to taste, and whisk for about 10 seconds to blend. Slowly whisk in the oil .

5 Add the lemon juice, spring onions, capers, pickles and parsley, and mix well. Check the seasoning. Cover and chill.

6 Preheat the grill. Brush the crab cakes with the olive oil. Place on an oiled baking sheet, in one layer.

7 Grill 15cm/6in from the heat until golden brown, about 5 minutes on each side. Serve the crab cakes with the tartare sauce, garnished with salad leaves, chives and lemon.

COOK'S TIP

For easier handling and to make the crab meat go further, add 50g/2oz/1 cup fresh breadcrumbs and 1 more egg to the crab mixture. Divide the mixture into 12 cakes to serve 6.

Scallops Wrapped in Parma Ham

Cook these lovely skewers on the barbecue for al fresco *summer dining. Serve with lime wedges for a sharper flavour.*

Serves 4

24 shucked medium-size scallops, corals removed

lemon juice

8–12 Parma ham slices, cut lengthways into 2 or 3 strips

olive oil, for brushing

ground black pepper

lemon wedges, to serve

1 Prepare the barbecue well in advance or preheat the grill when you make the skewers.

2 Sprinkle the scallops with lemon juice. Wrap a strip of Parma ham around each scallop. Thread on to 8 skewers.

3 Brush with oil. Arrange on a baking sheet if grilling. Grill about 10cm/4in from the heat, or cook over the barbecue, for 3–5 minutes on each side or until the scallops are opaque.

4 Set 2 skewers on each plate. Sprinkle the scallops with freshly ground black pepper and serve with lemon wedges.

COOK'S TIP

Use a short sturdy knife to pry shelled scallops open. Discard the membrane, organs and gristle at the side of the white meat. Set the coral aside. Rinse well.

Mussels and Clams with Lemon Grass

Lemon grass has an incomparable flavour and is excellent used with seafood. If you cannot find clams, use extra mussels instead.

INGREDIENTS

Serves 6

1.8–2kg/4–4½ lb mussels
450g/1lb baby clams, washed
120ml/4fl oz/½ cup dry white wine
1 bunch spring onions, chopped
2 lemon grass stalks, chopped
6 kaffir lime leaves, chopped
10ml/2 tsp Thai green curry paste
200ml/7fl oz/scant 1 cup coconut cream
30ml/2 tbsp chopped fresh coriander
salt and ground black pepper
whole garlic chives, to garnish

1 Clean the mussels. Pull off the beards and scrub the shells. Discard any that are broken or stay open when tapped.

2 Put the wine, spring onions, lemon grass, lime leaves and curry paste in a pan. Simmer until the wine almost evaporates.

3 Add the mussels and clams to the pan, cover tightly and steam the shellfish over a high heat for 5–6 minutes, until they open.

4 Using a slotted spoon, transfer the mussels and clams to a warmed serving bowl and keep hot. Discard any shellfish that remain closed. Strain the cooking liquid into a clean saucepan and then simmer to reduce the amount to about 250ml/8fl oz/1 cup.

5 Stir in the coconut cream and coriander, with salt and pepper to taste. Heat through. Pour over the seafood and serve, garnished with garlic chives.

COOK'S TIP

Buy a few extra mussels just in case there are any which have to be discarded.

Prawn Cocktail

There is no nicer starter than a good, fresh prawn cocktail – and nothing nastier than one in which soggy prawns swim in a thin, vinegary sauce embedded in limp lettuce. This recipe shows just how good a prawn cocktail can be.

INGREDIENTS

Serves 6

60ml/4 tbsp double cream, lightly whipped

60ml/4 tbsp mayonnaise, preferably home-made

60ml/4 tbsp tomato ketchup

5–10ml/1–2 tsp Worcestershire sauce

juice of 1 lemon

½ cos lettuce or other very crisp lettuce

450g/1lb/4 cups cooked peeled prawns

salt, ground black pepper and paprika

6 large whole cooked unpeeled prawns, to garnish (optional)

thinly sliced brown bread and lemon wedges, to serve

1 In a bowl, mix together the whipped cream, mayonnaise and ketchup. Add Worcestershire sauce to taste. Stir in enough lemon juice to make a really tangy cocktail sauce.

2 Finely shred the lettuce and fill six individual glasses one-third full. Stir the prawns into the sauce, then check the seasoning. Spoon the prawn mixture generously over the lettuce.

3 If you like, drape a whole cooked prawn over the edge of each glass (see Cook's Tip). Sprinkle each of the cocktails with ground black pepper and some paprika. Serve immediately, with thinly sliced brown bread and butter and lemon wedges for squeezing over.

COOK'S TIP

To prepare the garnish, peel the body shell from the prawns and leave the tail "fan" for decoration.

Aromatic Tiger Prawns

There is no elegant way to eat these aromatic prawns – just hold them by the tails, pull them off the sticks with your fingers and pop them into your mouth.

INGREDIENTS

Serves 4

16 raw tiger prawns or scampi tails

2.5ml/½ tsp chilli powder

5ml/1 tsp fennel seeds

5 Sichuan or black peppercorns

1 star anise, broken into segments

1 cinnamon stick, broken into pieces

30ml/2 tbsp groundnut or sunflower oil

2 garlic cloves, chopped

2cm/¾in piece fresh root ginger, peeled and finely chopped

1 shallot, chopped

30ml/2 tbsp water

30ml/2 tbsp rice vinegar

30ml/2 tbsp soft brown or palm sugar

salt and ground black pepper

lime slices and chopped spring onion, to garnish

1 Thread the prawns or scampi tails in pairs on 8 wooden cocktail sticks. Set aside. Heat a frying pan, put in all the chilli powder, fennel seeds, Sichuan or black peppercorns, star anise and cinnamon stick and dry-fry for 1–2 minutes to release the flavours. Leave to cool, then grind coarsely in a grinder or tip into a mortar and crush with a pestle.

2 Heat the groundnut or sunflower oil in a shallow pan, add the garlic, ginger and chopped shallot and then fry gently until very lightly coloured. Add the crushed spices and seasoning and cook the mixture gently for 2 minutes. Pour in the water and simmer, stirring, for 5 minutes.

3 Add the rice vinegar and soft brown or palm sugar, stir until dissolved, then add the prawns or scampi tails. Cook for about 3–5 minutes, until the seafood has turned pink, but is still very juicy. Serve hot, garnished with lime slices and spring onion.

> ### COOK'S TIP
> If you buy whole prawns, remove the heads before cooking them.

Salmon and Scallop Brochettes

With their delicate colours and really superb flavour, these skewers make the perfect opener for a sophisticated dinner party.

Serves 4

8 lemon grass stalks

225g/8oz salmon fillet, skinned

8 shucked queen scallops, with their corals
    if possible

8 baby onions, peeled and blanched

½ yellow pepper, cut into 8 squares

25g/1oz/2 tbsp butter

juice of ½ lemon

salt, ground white pepper and paprika

For the sauce

30ml/2 tbsp dry vermouth

50g/2oz/¼ cup butter

5ml/1 tsp chopped fresh tarragon

1 Preheat the grill to medium-high. Cut off the top 7.5–10cm/3–4in of each lemon grass stalk. Reserve the bulb ends for another dish. Cut the salmon fillet into twelve 2cm/¾ in cubes. Thread the salmon, scallops, corals if available, onions and pepper squares on to the lemon grass and arrange the brochettes in a grill pan.

2 Melt the butter in a small pan, add the lemon juice and a pinch of paprika and then brush all over the brochettes. Grill the skewers for about 2–3 minutes on each side, turning and basting the brochettes every minute, until the fish and scallops are just cooked, but are still very juicy. Transfer to a platter and keep hot while you make the tarragon butter sauce.

3 Pour the dry vermouth and the leftover cooking juices from the brochettes into a small pan and boil fiercely to reduce by half. Add the butter and melt, then stir in the chopped fresh tarragon and salt and ground white pepper to taste. Pour the tarragon butter sauce over the brochettes and serve.

Marinated Asparagus and Langoustine

For a really extravagant treat, you could make this attractive salad with medallions of lobster. For a cheaper version, use large prawns, allowing six per serving.

INGREDIENTS

Serves 4

16 langoustines

16 fresh asparagus spears, trimmed

2 carrots

30ml/2 tbsp olive oil

1 garlic clove, peeled

salt and ground black pepper

4 fresh tarragon sprigs and some chopped, to garnish

For the dressing

30ml/2 tbsp tarragon vinegar

120ml/4fl oz/½ cup olive oil

1 Peel the langoustines and keep the discarded parts for stock. Set aside.

2 Steam the asparagus over boiling salted water until just tender, but still a little crisp. Refresh under cold water, drain and place in a shallow dish.

3 Peel the carrots and cut into fine julienne shreds. Cook in a pan of lightly salted boiling water for about 3 minutes, until tender but still crunchy. Drain, refresh under cold water, drain again. Add to the asparagus.

4 Make the dressing. In a jug, whisk the tarragon vinegar with the oil. Season to taste. Pour over the asparagus and carrots and leave to marinate.

5 Heat the oil with the garlic in a frying pan until very hot. Add the langoustines and sauté quickly until just heated through. Discard the garlic.

6 Arrange four asparagus spears and the carrots on four individual plates. Drizzle over the dressing left in the dish and top each portion with four langoustine tails. Top with the tarragon sprigs and scatter the chopped tarragon on top. Serve immediately.

COOK'S TIP

Most of the langoustines we buy have been cooked at sea, a necessary act because the flesh deteriorates rapidly after death. Bear this in mind when you cook the shellfish. Because it has already been cooked, it will only need to be lightly sautéed until heated through. If you are lucky enough to buy live langoustines, kill them quickly by immersing them in boiling water, then sauté until cooked through.

Grilled Scallops with Brown Butter

This is a very striking dish as the scallops are served on the half shell, still sizzling from the grill. Reserve it for a very special occasion.

Serves 4

50g/2oz/¼ cup unsalted butter, diced

8 scallops, prepared on the half shell

15ml/1 tbsp chopped fresh parsley

salt and ground black pepper

lemon wedges, to serve

COOK'S TIP

∾

If you can't get hold of scallops in their shells, you can use shelled, fresh scallops if you cook them on the day of purchase.

1 Preheat the grill to high. Melt the butter in a small saucepan over a medium heat until it is pale golden brown. Remove the pan from the heat immediately; the butter must not be allowed to burn. Arrange the scallop shells in a single layer in a casserole or a shallow roasting pan. Brush a little of the brown butter over them.

2 Grill the scallops for 4 minutes – it will not be necessary to turn them. Pour over the remaining brown butter, then sprinkle a little salt and pepper and the parsley over. Serve immediately, with lemon wedges for squeezing over.

Fried Squid

The squid is simply dusted in flour and dipped in egg before being fried, so the coating is light and does not mask the flavour.

Serves 2

115g/4oz prepared squid, cut into rings

30ml/2 tbsp seasoned plain flour

1 egg

30ml/2 tbsp milk

olive oil, for frying

sea salt, to taste

lemon wedges, to serve

COOK'S TIP

∾

For a crisper coating, dust the rings in flour, then dip them in batter instead of this simple egg and flour coating.

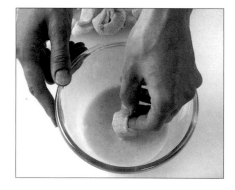

1 Toss the squid rings in the seasoned flour in a bowl or strong polythene bag. Beat the egg and milk together in a shallow bowl. Heat the oil in a heavy-based frying pan.

2 Dip the floured squid rings one at a time into the egg mixture, shaking off any excess liquid. Add to the hot oil, in batches if necessary, and fry for 2–3 minutes on each side until evenly golden all over.

3 Drain the fried squid on paper towels, then sprinkle with salt. Transfer to a small warm plate and serve with the lemon wedges.

Scallop and Mussel Kebabs

These delightfully crispy seafood skewers are served with hot toast spread with a lovely fresh herb butter.

INGREDIENTS

Serves 4

65g/2½oz/5 tbsp butter, at room temperature
30ml/2 tbsp minced fresh fennel or parsley
15ml/1 tbsp lemon juice
32 small scallops
24 large mussels, in the shell
8 bacon rashers
50g/2oz/1 cup fresh breadcrumbs
50ml/2fl oz/¼ cup olive oil
salt and ground black pepper
hot toast, to serve

3 Scrub the mussels well and remove their beards, then rinse under cold running water. Place in a large saucepan with about 2.5cm/1in of water in the base. Cover and steam the mussels over a medium heat until they open. When cool enough to handle, remove them from their shells, and pat dry using kitchen paper. Discard any mussels that have not opened during cooking.

4 Take 8 15cm/6in wooden or metal skewers. Thread on each one, alternately, 4 scallops and 3 mussels. As you are doing this, weave a rasher of bacon between the scallops and mussels.

5 Preheat the grill. Spread the breadcrumbs on a plate. Brush the seafood with olive oil and roll in the crumbs to coat all over.

6 Place the skewers on the grill rack. Grill until crisp and lightly browned, 4–5 minutes on each side. Serve immediately with hot toast and the flavoured butter.

1 Make the flavoured butter by combining the butter with the minced herbs and lemon juice. Add salt and pepper to taste. Mix well and set aside.

2 In a small saucepan, cook the scallops in their own liquor until they begin to shrink. (If there is no scallop liquor – retained from the shells after shucking – use a little fish stock or white wine.) Drain the scallops well and then pat dry with kitchen paper.

Monkfish Packages

Notoriously ugly, the monkfish makes delicious eating with its faintly shellfish-like flavour. You could use a cheaper fish but you'll lose that taste.

INGREDIENTS

Serves 4

175g/6oz/1½ cups bread flour
2 eggs
115g/4oz skinless monkfish fillet, diced
grated rind of 1 lemon
1 garlic clove, chopped
1 small red chilli, seeded and sliced
45ml/3 tbsp chopped fresh parsley
30ml/2 tbsp single cream
salt and ground black pepper

For the tomato oil

2 tomatoes, peeled, seeded and
   finely diced
45ml/3 tbsp extra virgin olive oil
15ml/1 tbsp lemon juice

1 Place the bread flour, eggs and 2.5ml/½ tsp salt in a blender or food processor; pulse until it forms a soft dough. Knead for 2–3 minutes. Wrap in clear film and chill for 20 minutes.

2 Place the monkfish, lemon rind, garlic, chilli and parsley in the clean food processor; process until very finely chopped. Add the cream, with plenty of salt and ground black pepper, and process again until a very thick paste is formed.

3 Make the tomato oil by stirring the diced tomatoes with the olive oil and lemon juice in a bowl. Add salt to taste. Cover and chill.

COOK'S TIP
❧
If the dough is sticky, sprinkle a little flour into the bowl of the food processor.

4 Roll out the dough thinly on a lightly floured surface and cut out 32 rounds, using a 4cm/1½in plain cutter. Divide the filling among half the rounds, then cover with the remaining rounds. Pinch the edges tightly to seal, trying to exclude as much air as possible.

5 Bring a large saucepan of water to a simmer and poach the fish packages in batches, for 2–3 minutes, or until they rise to the surface. Drain and serve hot, drizzled with the tomato oil.

SALADS

Pear and Parmesan Salad

This is a good starter when pears are at their seasonal best. Try Packhams or Comice when plentiful, drizzled with a poppy-seed dressing and topped with shavings of Parmesan.

Serves 4

4 just-ripe dessert pears

50g/2oz piece Parmesan cheese

watercress, to garnish

water biscuits or rye bread, to
   serve (optional)

For the dressing

30ml/2 tbsp extra virgin olive oil

15ml/1 tbsp sunflower oil

30ml/2 tbsp cider vinegar or white
   wine vinegar

2.5ml/½ tsp soft light brown sugar

good pinch of dried thyme

15ml/1 tbsp poppy seeds

salt and ground black pepper

1 Cut the pears in quarters and remove the cores. Cut each pear quarter in half lengthways and arrange them on four small serving plates. Peel the pears if you wish, though they look more attractive unpeeled.

2 Make the dressing. Mix the oils, vinegar, sugar, thyme and seasoning in a jug. Whisk well, then tip in the poppy seeds. Trickle the dressing over the pears. Garnish with watercress and shave Parmesan over the top. Serve with water biscuits or thinly sliced rye bread, if you like.

COOK'S TIP

∾

Blue cheeses and pears also have a natural affinity Stilton, dolcelatte, Gorgonzola or Danish blue are good substitutes. Allow about 200g/7oz and cut into wedges or cubes. This makes a slightly more substantial first course, so follow with a light dish.

Panzanella Salad

If sliced juicy tomatoes layered with day-old bread sounds strange for a salad, don't be deceived – it's quite delicious. A popular Italian salad, this dish is ideal for serving as a starter. Use full-flavoured tomatoes for the best result.

INGREDIENTS

Serves 4–6

4 thick slices day-old bread, either white,
   brown or rye

1 small red onion, thinly sliced

450g/1lb ripe tomatoes, thinly sliced

115g/4oz mozzarella cheese, thinly sliced

5ml/1 tbsp fresh basil, shredded, or
   fresh marjoram

120ml/4fl oz/½ cup extra virgin olive oil

45ml/3 tbsp balsamic vinegar

juice or 1 small lemon

salt and ground black pepper

stoned and sliced black olives or salted
   capers, to garnish

1 Dip the bread briefly in cold water, then carefully squeeze out the excess water. Arrange the bread in the base of a shallow salad bowl.

2 Soak the onion slices in cold water for about 10 minutes while you prepare the other ingredients. Drain and reserve.

3 Layer the tomatoes, cheese, onion, basil or marjoram, seasoning well in between each layer. Sprinkle with oil, vinegar and lemon juice.

4 Top with the olives or capers, cover with clear film and chill in the fridge for at least 2 hours or overnight, if possible.

Orange and Red Onion Salad with Cumin

Cumin and mint give this refreshing starter a Middle Eastern flavour. Choose small seedless oranges.

Serves 6

6 oranges

2 red onions

15ml/1 tbsp cumin seeds

5ml/1 tsp coarsely ground black pepper

15ml/1 tbsp chopped fresh mint

90ml/6 tbsp olive oil

salt

To serve

fresh mint sprigs

black olives

1 Slice the oranges thinly, working over a bowl to catch any juice. Then, holding each orange slice in turn over the bowl, cut round with scissors to remove the peel and pith. Slice the onions thinly and separate the rings.

2 Arrange the orange and onion slices in layers in a shallow dish, sprinkling each layer with cumin seeds, black pepper, mint, olive oil and salt to taste. Pour over the orange juice collected when slicing the oranges.

3 Leave the salad to marinate in a cool place for about 2 hours. Just before serving, scatter the salad with the mint sprigs and black olives.

Spanish Salad with Olives and Capers

Make this refreshing salad in the summer when tomatoes are sweet and full of flavour. The dressing gives it a lovely tang.

Serves 4

4 tomatoes

½ cucumber

1 bunch spring onions

1 bunch purslane or watercress, washed

8 pimiento-stuffed olives

30ml/2 tbsp drained capers

Dressing

30ml/2 tbsp red wine vinegar

5ml/1 tsp paprika

2.5ml/½ tsp ground cumin

1 garlic clove, crushed

75ml/5 tbsp olive oil

salt and ground black pepper

1 To peel the tomatoes, place them in a heatproof bowl, add boiling water to cover and leave for 1 minute. Lift out with a slotted spoon and plunge into a bowl of cold water. Leave for 1 minute, then drain. Slip the skins off the tomatoes and dice the flesh finely. Put in a salad bowl.

2 Peel the cucumber, dice it finely and add it to the tomatoes. Trim and chop half the spring onions, add them to the salad bowl and mix lightly.

3 Break the purslane or watercress into small sprigs. Add to the tomato mixture, with the olives and capers.

4 Make the dressing. Mix the wine vinegar, paprika, cumin and garlic in a bowl. Whisk in the oil and add salt and pepper to taste. Pour over the salad and toss lightly to coat. Serve with the remaining spring onions on the side.

Caesar Salad

This is a well-known and much enjoyed salad, even though its origins are a mystery. Be sure to use cos lettuce and add the very soft eggs at the last minute.

INGREDIENTS

Serves 6

175ml/6fl oz/³⁄₄ cup salad oil, preferably olive oil

115g/4oz French or Italian bread, cut in 2.5cm/1in cubes

1 large garlic clove, crushed with the flat side of a knife

1 cos lettuce

2 eggs, boiled for 1 minute

120ml/4fl oz/¹⁄₂ cup lemon juice

50g/2oz/²⁄₃ cup freshly grated Parmesan cheese

6 anchovy fillets, drained and finely chopped (optional)

salt and ground black pepper

1 Heat 50ml/2fl oz/¹⁄₄ cup of the oil in a large frying pan. Add the bread cubes and garlic. Fry, stirring and turning constantly, until the cubes are golden brown all over. Drain on kitchen paper. Discard the garlic.

2 Tear large lettuce leaves into smaller pieces. Then put all the lettuce in a bowl.

3 Add the remaining oil to the lettuce and season with salt and plenty of ground black pepper. Toss well to coat the leaves.

4 Break the eggs on top. Sprinkle with the lemon juice. Toss well again to combine.

5 Add the Parmesan cheese and anchovies, if using. Toss gently to mix.

6 Scatter the fried bread cubes on top and serve immediately.

COOK'S TIP

To make a tangier dressing mix 30ml/2 tbsp white wine vinegar, 15ml/1 tbsp Worcestershire sauce, 2.5ml/¹⁄₂ tsp mustard powder, 5ml/1 tsp sugar, salt and pepper in a screw-top jar, then add the oil and shake well.

Tricolour Salad

A popular salad, this dish depends for its success on the quality of its ingredients. Mozzarella di bufala is the best cheese to serve uncooked. Whole ripe plum tomatoes give up their juice to blend with extra virgin olive oil for a natural dressing.

INGREDIENTS

Serves 2–3

150g/5oz mozzarella di bufala cheese, thinly sliced

4 large plum tomatoes, sliced

1 large avocado

about 12 basil leaves or a small handful of flat leaf parsley leaves

45–60ml/3–4 tbsp extra virgin olive oil

ground black pepper

ciabatta and sea salt flakes, to serve

1 Arrange the sliced mozzarella cheese and tomatoes randomly on two salad plates. Crush over a few good pinches of sea salt flakes. This will help to draw out some of the juices from the plum tomatoes. Set aside in a cool place and leave to marinate for about 30 minutes.

2 Just before serving, cut the avocado in half using a large sharp knife and twist the halves to separate. Lift out the stone and remove the peel.

3 Carefully slice the avocado flesh crossways into half moons, or cut it into large chunks if that is easier.

4 Place the avocado on the salad, then sprinkle with the basil or parsley. Drizzle over the olive oil, add a little more salt if liked and some black pepper. Serve at room temperature, with chunks of crusty Italian ciabatta for mopping up the dressing.

Warm Broad Bean and Feta Salad

This recipe is loosely based on a typical medley of fresh-tasting Greek salad ingredients – broad beans, tomatoes and feta cheese. It's lovely as a starter, served warm or cold.

INGREDIENTS

Serves 4–6

900g/2lb broad beans, shelled, or
   350g/12oz shelled frozen beans

60ml/4 tbsp olive oil

75g/3oz plum tomatoes, halved, or
   quartered if large

4 garlic cloves, crushed

115g/4oz firm feta cheese, cut into large,
   even-size chunks

45ml/3 tbsp chopped fresh dill, plus extra
   to garnish

12 black olives

salt and ground black pepper

1 Cook the fresh or frozen broad beans in boiling, salted water until just tender. Drain and refresh, then set aside.

2 Meanwhile, heat the oil in a heavy-based frying pan and add the tomatoes and garlic. Cook until the tomatoes are beginning to colour.

3 Add the feta to the pan and toss the ingredients together for 1 minute. Mix with the drained beans, dill, olives and salt and pepper. Serve garnished with chopped dill.

Halloumi and Grape Salad

In Eastern Europe, firm salty halloumi cheese is often served fried for breakfast or supper. In this recipe for an unusual starter it's tossed with sweet, juicy grapes which really complement its distinctive sweet and salty flavour.

INGREDIENTS

Serves 4

150g/5oz mixed green salad leaves

75g/3oz seedless green grapes

75g/3oz seedless black grapes

250g/9oz halloumi cheese

45ml/3 tbsp olive oil

fresh young thyme leaves or dill,
   to garnish

For the Dressing

60ml/4 tbsp olive oil

15ml/1 tbsp lemon juice

2.5ml/½ tsp caster sugar

salt and ground black pepper

5ml/1 tsp chopped fresh thyme or dill

1 To make the dressing, mix together the olive oil, lemon juice and sugar. Season with salt and ground black pepper. Stir in the thyme or dill and set aside.

2 Toss together the salad leaves and the green and black grapes, then transfer to a large serving plate.

3 Thinly slice the cheese. Heat the oil in a large frying pan. Add the cheese and fry briefly until turning golden on the underside. Turn the cheese with a fish slice and cook the other side.

4 Arrange the cheese over the salad. Pour over the dressing and garnish with thyme or dill.

Asparagus and Orange Salad

A simple dressing of olive oil and vinegar mingles with the orange and tomato flavours with great results.

INGREDIENTS

Serves 4

225g/8oz asparagus, trimmed and cut into
   5cm/2in pieces
2 large oranges
2 well-flavoured ripe tomatoes, cut
   into eighths
50g/2oz romaine lettuce leaves, shredded
30ml/2 tbsp extra virgin olive oil
2.5ml/½ tsp sherry vinegar
salt and ground black pepper

1 Cook the asparagus in boiling, salted water for 3–4 minutes, until just tender. Drain and refresh under cold water. Set aside.

2 Grate the rind from half an orange and reserve. Peel all the oranges and cut into segments, leaving the membrane behind. Squeeze out the juice from the membrane and reserve the juice.

3 Put the asparagus, orange segments, tomatoes and lettuce into a salad bowl. Mix together the oil and vinegar and add 15ml/1 tbsp of the reserved orange juice and 5ml/1 tsp of the rind. Season with salt and plenty of ground black pepper. Just before serving, pour the dressing over the salad and mix gently to coat.

Salade Niçoise

*Made with the freshest ingredients,
this classic Provençal salad makes
a simple yet unbeatable summer
dish. Serve with country-style bread
and chilled white wine for a
substantial starter.*

INGREDIENTS

Serves 4–6

115g/4oz French beans

1 tuna steak, about 175g/6oz

olive oil, for brushing

115g/4oz mixed salad leaves

½ small cucumber, thinly sliced

4 ripe tomatoes, quartered

50g/2oz can anchovies, drained and
    halved lengthways

4 hard-boiled eggs, quartered

½ bunch radishes, trimmed

50g/2oz/½ cup small black olives

salt and ground black pepper

flat leaf parsley, to garnish

For the dressing

90ml/6 tbsp virgin olive oil

2 garlic cloves, crushed

15ml/1 tbsp white wine vinegar

salt and ground black pepper

1 Whisk together the oil, garlic
and vinegar then season to
taste with salt and pepper.

2 Preheat the grill. Brush the
tuna steak with olive oil and
season with salt and black pepper.
Grill for 3–4 minutes on each side
until cooked through. Set aside
and leave to cool.

3 Trim and halve theFrench
beans. Cook them in a pan of
boiling water for 2 minutes until
only just tender, then drain, refresh
and leave to cool.

4 Mix together the salad leaves,
sliced cucumber, tomatoes and
French beans in a large, shallow
bowl. Flake the tuna steak with
your fingers or two forks.

5 Scatter the tuna, anchovies,
eggs, radishes and olives over
the salad. Pour over the dressing
and toss together lightly. Serve
garnished with parsley.

Pear and Roquefort Salad

Choose ripe, firm Comice or Williams pears for this salad.

Serves 4

3 ripe pears

lemon juice, for tossing

about 175g/6oz mixed salad leaves

175g/6oz Roquefort cheese

50g/2oz/½ cup hazelnut kernels, toasted
  and chopped

For the dressing

30ml/2 tbsp hazelnut oil

45ml/3 tbsp olive oil

15ml/1 tbsp cider vinegar

5ml/1 tsp Dijon mustard

salt and ground black pepper

1 To make the dressing, mix together the oils, vinegar and mustard in a bowl or screw-top jar. Add salt and black pepper to taste. Stir or shake well.

2 Peel, core and slice the pears and toss them in lemon juice.

3 Arrange the salad leaves on serving plates, then place the pears on top. Crumble the cheese and scatter over the salad with the hazelnuts. Spoon over the dressing and serve at once.

Green Bean and Sweet Red Pepper Salad

Serrano chillies are very fiery so be cautious about their use.

INGREDIENTS

Serves 4

350g/12oz cooked green beans, quartered

2 red peppers, seeded and chopped

2 spring onions, chopped

1 or more drained pickled serrano chillies, rinsed, seeded and chopped

1 iceberg lettuce, coarsely shredded

olives, to garnish

For the dressing

45ml/3 tbsp red wine vinegar

135ml/9 tbsp olive oil

salt and ground black pepper

1 Combine the cooked green beans, chopped peppers, chopped spring onions and chillies in a salad bowl.

2 Make the salad dressing. Pour the red wine vinegar into a bowl or jug. Add salt and ground black pepper to taste, then gradually whisk in the olive oil until well combined.

3 Pour the salad dressing over the prepared vegetables and toss lightly together to mix and coat thoroughly.

4 Line a large serving platter with the shredded iceberg lettuce leaves and arrange the salad vegetables attractively on top. Garnish with the olives and serve

Wilted Spinach and Bacon Salad

The hot dressing in this salad wilts the spinach and provides a taste sensation.

INGREDIENTS

Serves 6

450g/1lb fresh young spinach leaves

225g/8oz streaky bacon rashers

25ml/1½ tbsp vegetable oil

60ml/4 tbsp red wine vinegar

60ml/4 tbsp water

20ml/4 tsp caster sugar

5ml/1 tsp dry mustard

8 spring onions, thinly sliced

6 radishes, thinly sliced

2 hard-boiled eggs, coarsely grated

salt and ground black pepper

1 Pull any coarse stalks from the spinach leaves and rinse well. Put the leaves in a large salad bowl.

2 Fry the bacon rashers in the oil until crisp and brown. Remove with tongs and drain on paper towels. Reserve the cooking fat in the pan. Chop the bacon and set aside until needed.

3 Combine the vinegar, water, sugar, mustard, and salt and ground black pepper in a bowl and stir until smoothly blended. Add to the fat in the frying pan and stir to mix. Bring the dressing to the boil, stirring.

4 Pour the hot dressing evenly over the spinach leaves. Scatter the bacon, spring onions, radishes and eggs over, and toss, then serve.

Melon and Parma Ham Salad

*Sections of cool fragrant melon
wrapped with slices of air-dried
ham make a delicious salad starter.
If strawberries are in season, serve
with a savoury-sweet strawberry
salsa and watch it disappear.*

INGREDIENTS

Serves 4

1 large melon, cantaloupe, charentais
 or galia
175g/6oz Parma or Serrano ham,
 thinly sliced

For the salsa

225g/8oz/2 cups strawberries
5ml/1 tsp caster sugar
30ml/2 tbsp groundnut or sunflower oil
15ml/1 tbsp orange juice
2.5ml/½ tsp finely grated orange rind
2.5ml/½ tsp finely grated fresh
 root ginger
salt and ground black pepper

1 Halve the melon and scoop the
seeds out with a spoon. Cut
the rind away with a paring knife,
then slice the melon thickly. Chill
until ready to serve.

2 To make the salsa, hull the
strawberries and cut them into
large dice. Place in a small mixing
bowl with the sugar and crush
lightly to release the juices. Add the
oil, orange juice, rind and ginger.
Season with salt and plenty of
ground black pepper.

3 Arrange the melon on a
serving plate, lay the ham over
the top and serve with a bowl of
salsa, handed round separately.

Roasted Tomato and Mozzarella Salad

Roasting the tomatoes brings out their sweetness and adds a new dimension to this salad. Make the basil oil just before serving to retain its fresh flavour and vivid colour.

Serves 4

6 large plum tomatoes

olive oil, for brushing

2 fresh mozzarella cheese balls, cut into
   8–12 slices

salt and ground black pepper

basil leaves, to garnish

For the basil oil

25 basil leaves

60ml/4 tbsp extra virgin olive oil

1 garlic clove, crushed

1 Preheat the oven to 200°C/ 400°F/Gas 6 and oil a baking tray. Cut the tomatoes in half lengthways and remove the seeds. Place the halves skin-side down on the baking tray and roast for 20 minutes or until the tomatoes are very tender but still retain their shape.

2 Meanwhile, make the basil oil. Place the basil leaves, olive oil and garlic in a food processor or blender and process until smooth. You will need to scrape down the sides once or twice to ensure the mixture is processed properly. Transfer to a bowl and chill until required.

3 For each serving, place the tomato halves on top of 2 or 3 slices of mozzarella and drizzle over the oil. Season well. Garnish with basil leaves and serve at once.

Mixed Herb Salad with Toasted Mixed Seeds

This simple salad is the perfect antidote to a rich, heavy meal as it contains fresh herbs that can ease the digestion. Balsamic vinegar adds a rich, sweet taste to the dressing, but red or white wine vinegar could be used instead.

Serves 4

90g/3½oz/4 cups mixed salad leaves

50g/2oz/2 cups mixed salad herbs, such as
   coriander, parsley, basil, chervil
   and rocket

25g/1oz/3 tbsp pumpkin seeds

25g/1oz/3 tbsp sunflower seeds

For the dressing

60ml/4 tbsp extra virgin olive oil

15ml/1 tbsp balsamic vinegar

2.5ml/½ tsp Dijon mustard

salt and ground black pepper

1 To make the dressing, combine the ingredients in a bowl or screw-top jar. Mix with a small whisk or fork, or shake well, until completely combined.

2 Put the salad leaves and herb leaves in a large bowl. Toss with your fingers to mix together.

3 Toast the pumpkin and sunflower seeds in a dry frying pan over a medium heat for about 2 minutes until golden, tossing frequently to prevent them burning. Allow the seeds to cool slightly before sprinkling them over the salad.

4 Pour the dressing over the salad and toss with your hands until the leaves are well coated, then serve.

Potato Salad with Curry Plant Mayonnaise

Potato salad can be made well in advance and is therefore a useful dish for serving as an unusual starter at a party. Its popularity means that there are very rarely any leftovers to be cleared away at the end of the day.

INGREDIENTS

Serves 6

1kg/2¼lb new potatoes, in skins

300ml/½ pint/1¼ cups shop-bought
   mayonnaise

6 curry plant leaves, roughly chopped

salt and ground black pepper

mixed lettuce leaves or other salad greens,
   to serve

1 Place the potatoes in a pan of salted water, bring to the boil and cook for 15 minutes or until tender. Drain and place in a large bowl to cool slightly.

2 Mix the mayonnaise with the curry plant leaves and black pepper. Stir these into the potatoes while they are still warm. Leave to cool completely, then serve on a bed of mixed lettuce leaves or other assorted salad leaves.

Avocado and Smoked Fish Salad

Avocado and smoked fish make a good combination, and flavoured with herbs and spices, create a delectable and elegant starter.

INGREDIENTS

Serves 4

15g/½oz/1 tbsp butter or margarine

½ onion, finely sliced

5ml/1 tsp mustard seeds

225g/8oz smoked mackerel, flaked

30ml/2 tbsp fresh chopped coriander

2 firm tomatoes, peeled and chopped

15ml/1 tbsp lemon juice

For the salad

2 avocados

½ cucumber

15ml/1 tbsp lemon juice

2 firm tomatoes

1 green chilli

salt and ground black pepper

1 Melt the butter or margarine in a frying pan, add the onion and mustard seeds and fry for about 5 minutes until the onion is soft but not browned.

2 Add the fish, chopped coriander, tomatoes and lemon juice and cook over a low heat for about 2–3 minutes. Remove from the heat and leave to cool.

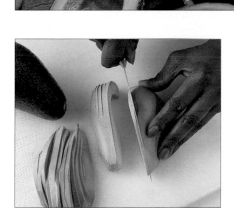

COOK'S TIP

Smoked mackerel has a distinctive flavour, but smoked haddock or cod can also be used in this salad, or a mixture of mackerel and haddock. For a speedy salad, canned tuna makes a convenient substitute.

3 To make the salad, slice the avocados and cucumber thinly. Place together in a bowl and sprinkle with the lemon juice to prevent discoloration.

4 Slice the tomatoes and seed and finely chop the chilli.

5 Place the fish mixture in the centre of a serving plate.

6 Arrange the avocado slices, cucumber and tomatoes decoratively around the outside of the fish. Alternatively, spoon a quarter of the fish mixture on to each of four serving plates and divide the avocados, cucumber and tomatoes equally among them. Then sprinkle with the chopped chilli and a little salt and ground black pepper, and serve.

Piquant Prawn Salad

The Thai-inspired dressing, which includes fish sauce and sesame oil, adds a superb flavour to the rice noodles and tiger prawns. This delicious salad can be served warm; or alternatively, chill before serving.

INGREDIENTS

Serves 6

200g/7oz rice vermicelli or stir-fry rice noodles

8 baby sweetcorn, halved

150g/5oz mangetouts

15ml/1 tbsp stir-fry oil

2 garlic cloves, finely chopped

2.5cm/1in piece fresh root ginger, peeled and finely chopped

1 fresh red or green chilli, seeded and finely chopped

450g/1lb raw peeled tiger prawns

4 spring onions, very thinly sliced

15ml/1 tbsp sesame seeds, toasted

1 lemon grass stalk, thinly shredded, to garnish

For the dressing

15ml/1 tbsp snipped fresh chives

15ml/1 tbsp *nam pla* (Thai fish sauce)

5ml/1 tsp soy sauce

45ml/3 tbsp groundnut oil

5ml/1 tsp sesame oil

30ml/2 tbsp rice vinegar

1 Put the rice vermicelli or noodles in a wide heatproof bowl, pour over boiling water and leave for 5 minutes. Drain, refresh under cold water and drain again. Tip back into the bowl and set aside until required.

2 Boil or steam the sweetcorn and mangetouts for about 3 minutes; they should still be crunchy. Refresh under cold water and drain. Now make the dressing. Mix all the ingredients in a screw-top jar, close tightly and shake well to combine.

3 Heat the oil in a large frying pan or wok. Add the garlic, ginger and red or green chilli and cook for 1 minute. Add the tiger prawns and stir-fry for 3 minutes, until they have just turned pink. Add the spring onions, sweetcorn, mangetouts and sesame seeds, and toss lightly to mix.

4 Tip the contents of the pan or wok over the rice vermicelli or noodles. Pour the dressing on top and toss well. Serve, garnished with lemon grass, or chill for an hour before serving.

Mushroom Salad with Parma Ham

Pancake ribbons create a lovely light texture to this starter. Use whatever edible wild mushrooms you can find, or substitute interesting cultivated varieties if you need to.

INGREDIENTS

Serves 4

40g/1½ oz/3 tbsp unsalted butter

450g/1lb assorted wild and cultivated
  mushrooms such as chanterelles, ceps,
  bay boletus, Caesar's mushrooms,
  oyster, field and Paris mushrooms,
  trimmed and sliced

60ml/4 tbsp Madeira or sherry

juice of ½ lemon

½ oak leaf lettuce

½ frisée lettuce

30ml/2 tbsp walnut oil

salt and ground black pepper

For the pancake and ham ribbons

25g/1oz/3 tbsp plain flour

75ml/5 tbsp milk

1 egg

60ml/4 tbsp freshly grated
  Parmesan cheese

60ml/4 tbsp chopped fresh herbs such as
  parsley, thyme, marjoram or chives

salt and pepper

butter, for frying

175g/6oz Parma ham, thickly sliced

1 To make the pancakes, blend the flour and the milk. Beat in the egg, cheese, herbs and some seasoning. Heat the butter in a frying pan and pour enough of the mixture to coat the base. When the batter has set, turn the pancake over and cook until firm.

2 Turn out and cool. Roll up the pancake and slice to make 1cm/½in ribbons. Cook the remaining batter the same way and cut the ham into similar sized ribbons. Toss with the pancake ribbons. Set aside.

3 Gently soften the mushrooms in the butter for 6–8 minutes until the moisture has evaporated. Add the Madeira or sherry and lemon juice; season.

4 Toss the salad leaves in the oil and arrange on four plates. Place the Parma ham and pancake ribbons in the centre, spoon on the mushrooms and serve.

Goat's Cheese Salad

Goat's cheese has a strong, tangy flavour so choose robust salad leaves to accompany it.

INGREDIENTS

Serves 4

30ml/2 tbsp olive oil

4 slices of French bread, 1cm/½ in thick

8 cups mixed salad leaves, such as curly endive, radicchio and red oak leaf, torn in small pieces

4 firm goat's cheese rounds, about 50g/2oz each, rind removed

1 yellow or red pepper, seeded and finely diced

1 small red onion, thinly sliced

45ml/3 tbsp chopped fresh parsley

30ml/2 tbsp snipped fresh chives

For the dressing

30ml/2 tbsp white wine vinegar

1.5ml/¼ tsp salt

5ml/1 tsp wholegrain mustard

75ml/5 tbsp olive oil

ground black pepper

1 For the dressing, mix the vinegar and salt with a fork until dissolved. Stir in the mustard. Gradually stir in the olive oil until blended. Season with pepper and set aside until needed.

2 Preheat the grill. Heat the oil in a skillet. When hot, add the bread slices and fry until golden, about 1 minute. Turn and cook on the other side, about 30 seconds more. Drain on kitchen paper and set aside.

3 Place the salad leaves in a bowl. Add 45ml/3 tbsp of the dressing and toss to coat well. Divide the dressed leaves among four salad plates.

4 Preheat the grill. Place the goat's cheeses, cut sides up, on a baking sheet and grill until bubbling and golden, about 1–2 minutes.

5 Set a goat's cheese on each slice of bread and place in the centre of each plate. Scatter the diced pepper, red onion, parsley and chives over the salad. Drizzle with the remaining dressing and serve.

Smoked Trout Pasta Salad

The little pasta shells catch the trout creating tasty mouthfuls.

Serves 8

15g/½oz/1 tbsp butter

175g/6oz/1 cup minced bulb fennel

6 spring onions, 2 minced and the rest
  thinly sliced

225g/8oz skinless smoked trout
  fillets, flaked

45ml/3 tbsp chopped fresh dill

120ml/4fl oz/½ cup mayonnaise

10ml/2 tsp fresh lemon juice

30ml/2 tbsp whipping cream

450g/1lb/4 cups small pasta shapes, such
  as conchiglie

salt and ground black pepper

dill sprigs, to garnish

1 Melt the butter in a small pan. Cook the fennel and minced onions for 3–5 minutes. Transfer to a large bowl and cool slightly.

2 Add the sliced spring onions, trout, dill, mayonnaise, lemon juice and cream. Season and mix.

3 Bring a large pan of water to the boil. Salt to taste and add the pasta. Cook according to the instructions on the packet until just *al dente*. Drain thoroughly and leave to cool.

4 Add the pasta to **the vegetable** and trout mixture **and toss to** coat evenly. Taste for **seasoning.** Serve the salad lightly **chilled or at** room temperature, garnished with sprigs of dill.

Mixed Seafood Salad

If you cannot find all the seafood included in this dish in fresh form, then it's all right to use a combination of fresh and frozen, but do use what is in season first.

INGREDIENTS

Serves 6–8

350g/12oz small squid
1 small onion, cut into quarters
1 bay leaf
200g/7oz unpeeled prawns
675g/1½lb fresh mussels, in the shell
450g/1lb small fresh clams
175ml/6fl oz/¾ cup white wine
1 fennel bulb

For the dressing
75ml/5 tbsp extra virgin olive oil
45ml/3 tbsp lemon juice
1 garlic clove, finely chopped
salt and ground black pepper

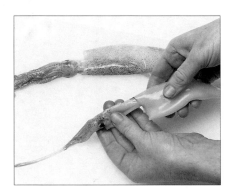

1 Working near the sink, clean the squid by first peeling off the thin skin from the body section. Rinse well. Pull the head and tentacles away from the sac section. Some of the intestines will come away with the head. Remove and discard the translucent quill and any remaining insides from the sac. Sever the tentacles from the head. Discard the head and intestines. Remove the small hard beak from the base of the tentacles. Rinse the sac and tentacles of the squid well under cold running water. Drain in a colander.

2 Bring a large pan of water to the boil. Add the onion and bay leaf. Drop in the squid and cook for about 10 minutes, or until tender. Remove with a draining spoon, and allow to cool before slicing into rings 1cm/½ in wide. Cut each tentacle section into 2 pieces. Set aside.

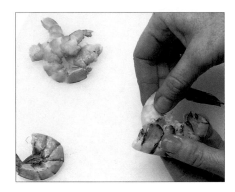

3 Drop the prawns into the same boiling water, and cook until they turn pink, about 2 minutes. Remove with a draining spoon. Peel and devein. (The cooking liquid may be strained and kept for using to make soup.) When cool, pop into the freezer if not using immediately.

4 Cut off the "beards" from the mussels. Scrub and rinse the mussels and clams well in several changes of cold water. Place in a large saucepan with the wine. Cover, and steam until all the shells have opened. (Discard any that do not open.) Lift the clams and mussels out.

5 Remove all the clams from their shells with a small spoon. Place in a large serving bowl. Remove all but 8 of the mussels from their shells, and add them to the clams in the bowl. Leave the remaining mussels in their half shells, and set aside. Cut the green, ferny part of the fennel away from the bulb. Chop finely and set aside. Chop the bulb into bite-size pieces, and add it to the serving bowl with the squid and prawns.

6 Make a dressing by combining the oil, lemon juice, garlic and chopped fennel green in a small bowl. Add salt and pepper to taste. Pour over the salad, and toss well. Decorate with the remaining mussels in the half shell. This salad may be served either at room temperature or lightly chilled.

Egg and Fennel Tabbouleh with Nuts

Tabbouleh is a Middle Eastern salad of steamed bulgur wheat, flavoured with lots of parsley, mint and garlic.

INGREDIENTS

Serves 4

250g/9oz/1¼ cups bulgur wheat
4 small eggs
1 fennel bulb
1 bunch spring onions, chopped
25g/1oz/½ cup sun-dried tomatoes, sliced
45ml/3 tbsp chopped fresh parsley
30ml/2 tbsp chopped fresh mint
75g/3oz/½ cup black olives
60ml/4 tbsp olive oil, preferably Greek
    or Spanish
30ml/2 tbsp garlic oil
30ml/2 tbsp lemon juice
salt and ground black pepper

1 Cover the bulgur wheat with boiling water and leave to soak for 15 minutes. Transfer to a metal sieve, place over a saucepan of boiling water, cover and steam for 10 minutes. Spread out on a metal tray and leave to cool while you cook the eggs and fennel.

2 Hard-boil the small eggs for 8 minutes. Cool under running water, peel and quarter, or, using an egg slicer, slice not quite all the way through.

3 Halve and then finely slice the fennel. Boil in salted water for 6 minutes, drain and cool under running water.

4 Combine the egg quarters, fennel, spring onions, sun-dried tomatoes, parsley, mint and olives with the bulgur wheat. If you have sliced the eggs, arrange them on top of the salad. Dress the tabbouleh with olive oil, garlic oil and lemon juice. Season well.

> ### COOK'S TIP
> ~
> Small whole eggs, such as gull, quail, plover or guinea fowl, would be good in this dish.

Ceviche

You can use almost any firm-fleshed fish for this South American dish, provided that is perfectly fresh. The fish is "cooked" by the action of the acidic lime juice. Adjust the amount of chilli according to your taste.

INGREDIENTS

Serves 6

675g/1½ lb halibut, turbot, sea bass or salmon fillets, skinned

juice of 3 limes

1–2 fresh red chillies, seeded and very finely chopped

15ml/1 tbsp olive oil

salt, to taste

For the garnish

4 large firm tomatoes, peeled, seeded and diced

1 ripe avocado, peeled and diced

15ml/1 tbsp lemon juice

30ml/2 tbsp olive oil

30ml/2 tbsp fresh coriander leaves

1 Cut the fish into strips measuring about 5 x 1cm/2 x ½in. Lay these in a shallow dish and pour over the lime juice, turning the fish strips to coat them all over in the juice. Cover with clear film and leave for 1 hour.

2 Meanwhile, prepare the garnish. Mix together all the ingredients except the coriander. Set aside.

3 Season the fish with salt and scatter over the chillies. Drizzle with the olive oil. Toss the fish in the mixture, then replace the cover. Leave to marinate in the fridge for 15–30 minutes more. To serve, divide the garnish among six plates. Arrange the ceviche, then sprinkle with coriander.

PARTY FINGER
FOOD

Cheese Aigrettes

Choux pastry is often associated with sweet pastries, such as profiteroles, but these little savoury buns, flavoured with Gruyère and dusted with grated Parmesan, are just delicious. They are best made ahead and deep-fried to serve. They make a wonderful party snack.

INGREDIENTS

Makes 30

90g/3½ oz/scant 1 cup strong plain flour

2.5ml/½ tsp paprika

2.5ml/½ tsp salt

75g/3oz/6 tbsp cold butter, diced

200ml/7fl oz/scant 1 cup water

3 eggs, beaten

75g/3oz mature Gruyère cheese,
   coarsely grated

corn or vegetable oil, for deep-frying

50g/2oz/⅔ cup freshly grated
   Parmesan cheese

ground black pepper

1 Mix the flour, paprika and salt together by sifting them on to a large sheet of greaseproof paper. Add a generous amount of ground black pepper.

2 Put the diced butter and water into a medium saucepan and heat gently. As soon as the butter has melted and the liquid starts to boil, quickly tip in all the seasoned flour at once and beat very hard with a wooden spoon until the dough comes away cleanly from the sides of the pan.

3 Remove the saucepan from the heat and cool the paste for 5 minutes. Gradually beat in enough of the beaten egg to give a stiff dropping consistency that still holds a shape on the spoon. Mix in the Gruyère.

4 Heat the oil for deep-frying to 180°C/350°F. Take a teaspoonful of the choux paste and use a second spoon to slide it into the oil. Make more aigrettes in the same way. Fry for 3–4 minutes then drain on kitchen paper and keep warm while cooking successive batches. To serve, pile the aigrettes on a warmed serving dish and sprinkle with Parmesan.

COOK'S TIP

Filling these aigrettes gives a delightful surprise as you bite through their crisp shell. Make slightly larger aigrettes by dropping a slightly larger spoonful of dough into the hot oil. Slit them open and scoop out any soft paste. Fill the centres with taramasalata or crumbled Roquefort mixed with a little fromage frais.

Parmesan Thins

These thin, crisp, savoury biscuits will melt in the mouth, so make plenty for guests. They are a great snack at any time of the day, so don't just keep them for parties.

INGREDIENTS

Makes 16–20

50g/2oz/½ cup plain flour

40g/1½ oz/3 tbsp butter, softened

1 egg yolk

40g/1½ oz/⅔ cup freshly grated
   Parmesan cheese

pinch of salt

pinch of mustard powder

1 Rub together the flour and the butter in a bowl using your fingertips, then work in the egg yolk, Parmesan cheese, salt and mustard. Mix to bring the dough together into a ball. Shape the mixture into a log, wrap in foil or clear film and chill in the fridge for 10 minutes.

2 Preheat the oven to 200°C/ 400°F/Gas 6. Cut the Parmesan log into very thin slices, 3–6mm/ ⅛–¼in maximum, and arrange on a baking sheet. Flatten with a fork to give a pretty ridged pattern. Bake for 10 minutes or until the biscuits are crisp but not changing colour.

Grilled Polenta with Gorgonzola

Grilled polenta is delicious, and is a good way of using up cold polenta. Try it with any soft flavoursome cheese. Here the polenta is cut into triangles but you could make different shapes if you like.

INGREDIENTS

Serves 6–8

1.5 litres/2½ pints/6¼ cups water

15ml/1 tbsp salt

350g/12oz/2½ cups polenta flour

225g/8oz/1¼ cups Gorgonzola or other
  cheese, at room temperature

1 Bring the water to the boil in a large heavy-based saucepan. Add the salt. Reduce the water to simmering, and begin to add the polenta flour in a fine rain. Stir constantly with a whisk until the polenta has all been incorporated.

2 Switch to a long-handled wooden spoon, and continue to stir the polenta over a low to moderate heat until it is a thick mass, and pulls away from the sides of the pan. This may take from 25–50 minutes, depending on the type of flour used. For best results, never stop stirring the polenta until you remove it from the heat.

3 When the polenta is cooked, sprinkle a work surface or large board with a little water. Spread the polenta out on the surface in a layer 2cm/¾in thick. Allow to cool completely. Preheat the grill.

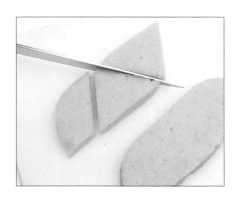

4 Cut the polenta into triangles. Grill until hot and speckled with brown on both sides. Spread with the Gorgonzola or other cheese. Serve immediately.

Cherry Tomatoes with Pesto

These make a colourful and tasty appetizer to go with drinks before you move to the table. Make the pesto when fresh basil is plentiful, and freeze it in batches.

INGREDIENTS

Serves 8–10

450g/1lb small cherry tomatoes

For the pesto

90g/3½ oz/1 cup fresh basil leaves

3–4 garlic cloves

60ml/4 tbsp pine nuts

5ml/1 tsp salt, plus extra to taste

120ml/4fl oz/½ cup olive oil

45ml/3 tbsp freshly grated
   Parmesan cheese

90ml/6 tbsp freshly grated
   pecorino cheese

ground black pepper

1 Wash the tomatoes. Slice off the top of each tomato, and carefully scoop out the seeds with a melon baller or small spoon.

2 Place the basil, garlic, pine nuts, salt and olive oil in a blender or food processor and process until smooth. Remove the contents to a bowl with a rubber spatula. If desired, the pesto may be frozen at this point, before the cheeses are added. To use when frozen, allow to thaw, then proceed to step 3.

3 Fold in the Parmesan and pecorino grated cheeses. Season with pepper, and more salt if necessary.

4 Use a small spoon to fill each tomato with a little pesto. This dish is at its best if chilled for about an hour before serving.

Spicy Peanut Balls

Tasty rice balls, rolled in chopped peanuts and deep-fried, make a delicious starter. Serve them as they are, or with a chilli sauce for dipping. Make sure there are plenty of napkins to hand.

INGREDIENTS

Makes 16

1 garlic clove, crushed

1cm/½ in piece fresh root ginger, peeled and finely chopped

1.5ml/¼ tsp turmeric

5ml/1 tsp granulated sugar

2.5ml/½ tsp salt

5ml/1 tsp chilli sauce

10ml/2 tsp fish sauce or soy sauce

30ml/2 tbsp chopped fresh coriander

juice of ½ lime

225g/8oz/2 cups cooked white long grain rice

115g/4oz/1 cup peanuts, chopped

vegetable oil, for deep-frying

lime wedges and chilli dipping sauce, to serve (optional)

1 Process the garlic, ginger and turmeric in a food processor or blender until the mixture forms a paste. Add the sugar, salt, chilli sauce and fish sauce or soy sauce, with the chopped coriander and lime juice. Process briefly to mix the ingredients.

2 Add three-quarters of the cooked rice to the paste in the and process until smooth and sticky. Scrape into a mixing bowl and stir in the remainder of the rice. Wet your hands and shape the mixture into thumb-size balls.

3 Roll the balls in the chopped peanuts, making sure they are evenly coated.

4 Heat the oil in a deep-fryer or wok. Deep-fry the peanut balls until crisp. Drain on kitchen paper and then pile on to a platter. Serve hot with lime wedges and a chilli dipping sauce, if using.

Eggs Mimosa

The use of the word mimosa describes the fine yellow and white grated egg which looks not unlike the flower of the same name. It can be used to finish any dish, adding a light summery touch.

INGREDIENTS

Serves 20

12 hard-boiled eggs, peeled

2 ripe avocados, halved and stoned

1 garlic clove, crushed

Tabasco sauce, to taste

15ml/1 tbsp virgin olive oil

salt and ground black pepper

20 chicory leaves or small crisp green
   lettuce leaves, to serve

basil leaves, to garnish

1 Reserve 2 eggs, halve the remainder and put the yolks in a mixing bowl. Blend or beat the yolks with the avocados, garlic, Tabasco sauce, oil and salt and pepper. Check the seasoning. Pipe or spoon this mixture back into the halved egg whites.

2 Sieve the remaining egg whites and sprinkle over the filled eggs. Sieve the yolks on top. Arrange each half egg on a chicory or lettuce leaf and place them on a serving platter. Scatter the shredded basil over the filled egg halves before serving.

Pickled Quail's Eggs

These Chinese eggs are pickled in alcohol and can be stored in a preserving jar in a cool dark place for several months. They will make delicious bite-size snacks at a drinks party and are sure to delight guests.

INGREDIENTS

Serves 12

12 quail's eggs

15ml/1 tbsp salt

750ml/1¼ pints/3 cups distilled or
    previously boiled water

15ml/1 tsp Sichuan peppercorns

150ml/¼ pint/⅔ cup spirit such as
    Mou-tal (Chinese brandy), brandy,
    whisky, rum or vodka

dipping sauce (see Cook's Tip) and
    toasted sesame seeds, to serve

1 Boil the eggs for about 4 minutes until the yolks are soft but not runny.

2 In a large saucepan, dissolve the salt in the distilled or previously boiled water. Add the peppercorns, then allow the water to cool and add the spirit.

3 Gently tap the eggs all over but do NOT peel them. Place in a large, airtight, sterilized jar and fill up with the liquid, totally covering the eggs. Seal the jar and leave the eggs to stand in a cool, dark place for 7–8 days.

4 To serve, remove the eggs from the liquid and peel off the shells carefully. Cut each egg in half or quarters and serve whole with a dipping sauce and a bowl of toasted sesame seeds.

COOK'S TIP

• Although you can buy Chinese dipping sauces in the supermarket, it is very easy to make your own at home. To make a quick dipping sauce, mix equal quantities of soy sauce and hoi-sin sauce.

• Be sure to use only boiled water or distilled water for the eggs, as the water must be completely free of bacteria or it will enter the porous shells.

Tandoori Chicken Sticks

This aromatic chicken dish is traditionally baked in a special clay oven called a tandoor. Here the chicken is grilled, with truly excellent results.

INGREDIENTS

Makes about 25

450g/1lb boneless, skinless chicken breasts

For the coriander yogurt

250ml/8fl oz/1 cup natural yogurt

30ml/2 tbsp whipping cream

½ cucumber, peeled, seeded and finely chopped

15–30ml/1–2 tbsp fresh chopped mint or coriander

salt and ground black pepper

For the marinade

175ml/6fl oz/¾ cup natural yogurt

5ml/1 tsp garam masala or curry powder

1.5ml/¼ tsp ground cumin

1.5ml/¼ tsp ground coriander

1.5ml/¼ tsp cayenne pepper (or to taste)

5ml/1 tsp tomato purée

1–2 garlic cloves, finely chopped

2.5cm/1in piece fresh root ginger, peeled and finely chopped

grated rind and juice of ½ lemon

15–30ml/1–2 tbsp chopped fresh mint or coriander

1 Prepare the coriander yogurt. Combine all the ingredients in a bowl and season with salt and ground black pepper. Cover with clear film and chill until you are ready to serve.

2 Prepare the marinade. Place all the ingredients in the bowl of a food processor, and process until the mixture is smooth. Pour into a shallow dish.

3 Freeze the chicken breasts for 5 minutes to firm, then slice in half horizontally. Cut the slices into 2cm/¾in strips and add to the marinade. Toss to coat well. Cover and chill in the fridge for 6–8 hours or overnight.

4 Preheat the grill and line a baking sheet with foil. Using a draining spoon, remove the chicken from the marinade and arrange the pieces in a single layer on the baking sheet. Scrunch up the chicken slightly so it makes wavy shapes. Grill for 4–5 minutes until brown and just cooked, turning once. When cool enough to handle, thread 1–2 pieces on to cocktail sticks or short skewers and serve with the coriander yogurt dip.

Stuffed Devilled Eggs

These eggs are so simple to make yet guests will always be impressed by them. They have a wonderful flavour and can be given quite a "kick" too by including the cayenne.

INGREDIENTS

Serves 6

6 hard-boiled eggs, peeled

40g/1½oz/¼ cup minced cooked ham

6 walnut halves, minced

15ml/1 tbsp minced spring onion

15ml/1 tbsp Dijon mustard

15ml/1 tbsp mayonnaise

10ml/2 tsp vinegar

1.5ml/¼ tsp salt

1.5ml/¼ tsp ground black pepper

1.5ml/¼ tsp cayenne pepper (optional)

paprika and a few gherkin slices,
    to garnish

1 Cut each hard-boiled egg in half lengthways. Put the yolks in a bowl and set the whites aside.

2 Mash the yolks well with a fork, or push them through a sieve. Add all the remaining ingredients except the garnish and mix well with the yolks. Taste and add more salt and pepper seasoning if necessary.

3 Spoon the filling into the egg white halves, or pipe it in with a pastry bag and nozzle. Garnish the top of each stuffed egg with a little paprika and a small star or other shape cut from the pickle slices. Serve the stuffed eggs at room temperature.

Stuffed Celery Sticks

The creamy filling contrasts well with the crunchy celery, and the walnuts add a wonderful flavour.

INGREDIENTS

Serves 4–6

12 crisp, tender celery stalks

25g/1oz/¼ cup crumbled blue cheese

115g/4oz/½ cup cream cheese

45ml/3 tbsp soured cream

50g/2oz/½ cup chopped walnuts

1 Trim the celery stalks. Wash them, if necessary, and dry well on kitchen paper. Cut into 10cm/4in lengths.

2 In a small bowl, combine the crumbled blue cheese, cream cheese and soured cream. Stir together with a wooden spoon until smoothly blended. Fold in all but 15ml/1 tbsp of the walnuts.

3 Fill the celery pieces with the cheese and nut mixture. Chill before serving, garnished with the reserved walnuts.

COOK'S TIP

Use the same filling to stuff scooped-out cherry tomatoes. Serve together if liked.

Tapenade and Quail's Eggs

Tapenade is a purée made from capers, olives and anchovies. It is popularly used in Mediterranean cooking. It complements the taste of eggs perfectly, especially quail's eggs, which look very pretty on open sandwiches.

INGREDIENTS

Serves 8

8 quail's eggs

1 small baguette

45ml/3 tbsp tapenade

curly endive leaves

3 small tomatoes, sliced

black olives

4 canned anchovy fillets, drained and
  halved lengthways

parsley sprigs, to garnish

1 Boil the quail's eggs for 3 minutes, then plunge them straight into cold water to cool. Crack the shells and remove them very carefully.

2 Cut the baguette into slices on the diagonal and spread each one with some of the tapenade.

3 Arrange a little curly endive, torn to fit, and the tomato slices on top.

4 Halve the quail's eggs and place them on top of the tomato slices.

5 Finish with a little more tapenade, the olives and finally the anchovies. Garnish with small parsley sprigs.

COOK'S TIP

To make 300ml/½ pint/1¼ cups of tuna tapenade, put a 90g/3½oz canned drained tuna in a food processor with 25g/1oz/2 tbsp capers, 10 canned anchovy fillets and 75g/3oz/¾ cup stoned black olives and blend until smooth, scraping down the sides as necessary. Gradually add 60ml/ 4 tbsp olive oil through the feeder tube. This purée can be used for filling hard-boiled eggs. Blend the tapenade with the egg yolks then pile into the whites.

Eggy Thai Fish Cakes

These tangy little fish cakes, with a kick of Eastern spice, make great party food, or made slightly larger, are a great starter too.

INGREDIENTS

Makes about 20

225g/8oz smoked cod or haddock (undyed)

225g/8oz fresh cod or haddock

1 small fresh red chilli, seeded and finely chopped

2 garlic cloves, grated

1 lemon grass stalk, very finely chopped

2 large spring onions, very finely chopped

30ml/2 tbsp Thai fish sauce (or 30ml/2 tbsp soy sauce and a few drops anchovy essence)

60ml/4 tbsp thick coconut milk

2 large eggs, lightly beaten

15ml/1 tbsp chopped fresh coriander

15ml/1 tbsp cornflour, plus extra for moulding

oil, for frying

soy sauce, rice vinegar or Thai fish sauce, for dipping

1 Place the prepared smoked fish in a bowl of cold water and leave to soak for 10 minutes. Dry well on kitchen paper. Chop the smoked and fresh fish roughly and place in a food processor.

2 Add the chilli, garlic, lemon grass, onions, the sauce and the coconut milk, and process until the fish is well blended with the spices. Add the eggs and coriander and process for a further few seconds. Cover with clear film and chill in the fridge for 1 hour.

3 To make the fish cakes, flour your hands with cornflour and shape large teaspoonfuls into neat balls, coating them with the flour.

4 Heat 5–7.5cm/2–3in oil in a medium pan until a crust of bread turns golden in about 1 minute. Fry the fish balls 5–6 at a time, turning them carefully with a slotted spoon for 2–3 minutes, until they turn golden all over. Remove with a slotted spoon and drain on kitchen paper. Keep the fish cakes warm in the oven until they are all cooked. Serve immediately with one or more dipping sauces.

Marinated Mussels

This is an ideal recipe to prepare and arrange well in advance. Remove from the fridge 15 minutes before serving to allow the flavours to develop fully.

Makes about 48

1kg/2¼lb mussels, large if possible
    (about 48)
175ml/6fl oz/¾ cup dry white wine
1 garlic clove, finely crushed
120ml/4fl oz/½ cup olive oil
50ml/2fl oz/¼ cup lemon juice
5ml/1 tsp hot chilli flakes
2.5ml/½ tsp mixed spice
15ml/1 tbsp Dijon mustard
10ml/2 tsp sugar
5ml/1 tsp salt
15–30ml/1–2 tbsp chopped fresh dill
    or coriander
15ml/1 tbsp capers, drained and chopped
    if large
ground black pepper

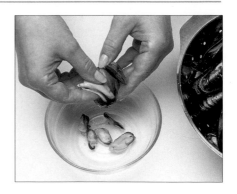

2 In a large casserole or pan set over a high heat, bring the white wine to the boil with the garlic and freshly ground black pepper. Add the mussels and cover. Reduce the heat to medium and simmer for 2–4 minutes until the shells open, stirring occasionally.

3 In a large bowl combine the olive oil, lemon juice, chilli flakes, mixed spice, Dijon mustard, sugar, salt, the chopped dill or coriander and the capers. Stir well then set aside.

4 Discard any mussels with closed shells. With a small sharp knife, carefully remove the remaining mussels from their shells, reserving the half shells for serving. Add the mussels to the marinade. Toss the mussels to coat well, then cover and chill in the fridge for 6–8 hours or overnight, stirring gently from time to time.

5 With a teaspoon, place one mussel with a little marinade in each shell. Arrange on a platter and cover until ready to serve.

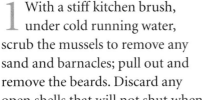

1 With a stiff kitchen brush, under cold running water, scrub the mussels to remove any sand and barnacles; pull out and remove the beards. Discard any open shells that will not shut when they are tapped.

COOK'S TIP

Mussels can be prepared ahead of time and marinated for up to 24 hours. To serve, arrange the mussel shells on a bed of crushed ice, well-washed seaweed or even coarse salt to stop them wobbling on the plate.

Sautéed Mussels with Garlic and Herbs

These mussels are served without their shells, in a delicious paprika-flavoured sauce. Eat them with cocktail sticks.

INGREDIENTS

Serves 4

900g/2lb fresh mussels
1 lemon slice
90ml/6 tbsp olive oil
2 shallots, finely chopped
1 garlic clove, finely chopped
15ml/1 tbsp chopped fresh parsley
2.5ml/½ tsp sweet paprika
1.5ml/¼ tsp dried chilli flakes

1 Scrub the mussels, discarding any damaged ones that do not close when tapped with a knife. Put the mussels in a large pan, with 250ml/8fl oz/1 cup water and the slice of lemon. Bring to the boil and cook for 3–4 minutes, removing the mussels as they open. Discard any that remain closed. Take the mussels out of the shells and drain on kitchen paper.

2 Heat the oil in a sauté pan, add the mussels and cook, stirring, for 1 minute. Remove from the pan. Add the shallots and garlic and cook, covered, over a low heat for about 5 minutes or until soft. Remove from the heat and stir in the parsley, paprika and chilli.

3 Return to the heat and stir in the mussels. Cook briefly. Remove from the heat and cover for a minute or two, to let the flavours mingle, before serving.

Prawn Toasts

These crunchy sesame-topped toasts are simple to prepare using a food processor for the prawn paste.

INGREDIENTS

Makes 64

225g/8oz cooked, peeled prawns, well drained and patted dry
1 egg white
2 spring onions, chopped
5ml/1 tsp chopped fresh root ginger
1 garlic clove, chopped
5ml/1 tsp cornflour
2.5ml/½ tsp salt
2.5ml/½ tsp sugar
2–3 dashes hot pepper sauce
8 slices firm-textured white bread
60–75ml/4–5 tbsp sesame seeds
vegetable oil, for frying
spring onion pompom, to garnish

1 Put the first 9 ingredients in the bowl of a food processor and process until the mixture forms a smooth paste, scraping down the side of the bowl from time to time.

COOK'S TIP

You can prepare these in advance and heat them through in a hot oven before serving. Make sure they are really crisp and hot though, because they won't be nearly so enjoyable if there's no crunch when you bite them!

2 Spread the prawn paste evenly over the bread slices, then sprinkle over the sesame seeds, pressing to make them stick. Remove the crusts, then cut each slice diagonally into 4 triangles, and each in half again. Make 64 triangles in total.

3 Heat 5cm/2in vegetable oil in a heavy saucepan or wok, until it is hot but not smoking. Fry the triangles in batches for about 30–60 seconds, turning the toasts once. Drain on paper towels and keep hot in the oven while you cook the rest. Serve hot with the garnish.

Tuna in Rolled Red Peppers

This lovely savoury combination originated in southern Italy. Grilled peppers have a sweet, smoky taste that combines particularly well with a robust fish like tuna. You could try canned mackerel instead.

Serves 8–10

3 large red peppers

200g/7oz can tuna fish, drained

30ml/2 tbsp lemon juice

45ml/3 tbsp olive oil

6 green or black olives, stoned and chopped

30ml/2 tbsp chopped fresh parsley

1 garlic clove, finely chopped

1 celery stalk, very finely chopped

salt and ground black pepper

1 Place the peppers under a hot grill, and turn occasionally until they are black and blistered on all sides. Remove from the heat and place in a polythene bag.

2 Leave for 5 minutes, and then peel. Cut the peppers into quarters, and remove the stems, seeds and pith.

3 Meanwhile, flake the tuna and combine with the lemon juice and oil. Stir in the olives, parsley, garlic and celery. Season with salt and plenty of ground black pepper.

4 Lay the pepper segments out flat, skin side down. Divide the tuna mixture equally among them. Spread it out, pressing it into an even layer. Roll the peppers up. Place the pepper rolls in the fridge for at least 1 hour. Just before serving, cut each roll in half with a sharp knife.

Smoked Trout Mousse in Cucumber Cups

This delicious creamy mousse can be made in advance and chilled for 2–3 days in the fridge. Serve it in crunchy cucumber cups, or simply with crudités if you prefer.

INGREDIENTS

Makes about 24

115g/4oz/½ cup cream cheese, softened

2 spring onions, chopped

15–30ml/1–2 tbsp, chopped fresh dill or parsley

5ml/1 tsp horseradish sauce

225g/8oz smoked trout fillets, flaked and any fine bones removed

30–60ml/2–4 tbsp double cream

salt, to taste

cayenne pepper, to taste

2 cucumbers

dill sprigs, to garnish

1 Put the cream cheese, spring onions, dill or parsley, and horseradish sauce into a blender or the bowl of a food processor and process until well blended. Add the trout and process until smooth, scraping down the sides of the bowl once. With the machine running, pour in the cream through the feeder tube until a soft mousse-like mixture forms. Season, turn into a bowl and chill for 15 minutes.

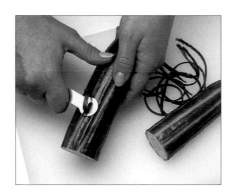

2 Using a canelle knife or vegetable peeler, score the length of each cucumber to create a striped effect. Cut each cucumber into 2cm/¾in thick rounds. Using a small spoon or melon baller, scoop out the seeds from the centre of each round.

3 Spoon the smoked trout mousse into a piping bag fitted with a medium star nozzle and pipe swirls of the mixture into the prepared cucumber rounds. Chill until ready to serve. Garnish the cucumber cups with small sprigs of dill.

Foie Gras Pâté in Filo Cups

This is an extravagantly rich hors d'oeuvre – so save it for a special anniversary or celebration.

INGREDIENTS

Makes 24

3–6 sheets fresh or defrosted filo pastry

40g/1½ oz/3 tbsp butter, melted

225g/8oz tinned foie gras pâté or other fine liver pâté, at room temperature

50g/2oz/4 tbsp butter, softened

30–45ml/2–3 tbsp Cognac or brandy (optional)

chopped pistachio nuts, to garnish

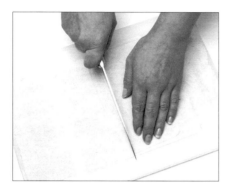

1 Preheat the oven to 200°C/ 400°F/Gas 6. Grease a bun tray with 24 x 4cm/1½in cups. Stack the filo sheets on a work surface and cut into 6cm/2½in squares. Cover with a damp dish towel.

2 Keeping the rest of the filo squares covered, place one square on a work surface and brush lightly with melted butter, then turn and brush the other side.

3 Butter a second square and place it over the first at an angle. Butter a third square and place at an angle over the first two sheets to form an uneven edge.

4 Press the layers into a cup of the bun tray. Continue with the remaining pastry and butter until all the cups in the bun tray have been filled.

5 Bake the filo cups for about 4–6 minutes until crisp and golden, then remove and cool in the tray for 5 minutes. Carefully transfer each filo cup to a wire rack and leave to cool completely.

6 In a small bowl, beat the pâté with the softened butter until smooth and well blended. Add the Cognac or brandy to taste, if using. Spoon into a piping bag fitted with a medium star nozzle and pipe a swirl into each cup. Sprinkle with pistachio nuts. Chill until you are ready to serve.

COOK'S TIP

The pâté and pastry are best eaten soon after preparation. If preparing ahead of time and then chilling in the fridge, be sure to bring back to room temperature before serving.

Monti Cristo Triangles

These opulent little sandwiches are stuffed with ham, cheese and turkey, dipped in egg, then fried in butter and oil. They are rich, very filling – and very popular too.

INGREDIENTS

Makes 64

16 slices firm-textured thin-sliced
   white bread
120g/4oz/½ cup butter, softened
8 slices oak-smoked ham
45–60ml/3–4 tbsp wholegrain mustard
8 slices Gruyère or Emmenthal cheese
45–60ml/3–4 tbsp mayonnaise
8 slices turkey or chicken breast
4–5 eggs
50ml/2 fl oz/¼ cup milk
5ml/1 tsp Dijon mustard
vegetable oil, for frying
butter, for frying
salt and ground white pepper
pimiento-stuffed green olives, to garnish
parsley leaves, to garnish

1 Arrange 8 of the bread slices on a work surface and spread with half the softened butter. Lay a slice of ham on each slice of bread and spread with a little mustard. Cover with a slice of Gruyère or Emmenthal cheese and spread with a little of the mayonnaise, then cover with a slice of turkey or chicken breast. Butter the rest of the bread slices and use to top the sandwiches. Cut off the crusts, trimming to an even square.

2 In a large shallow baking dish, beat the eggs, milk and Dijon mustard until well combined. Season with salt and pepper. Soak the sandwiches in the egg mixture on both sides until the egg has been absorbed.

3 Heat about 1cm/½in of oil with a little butter in a large heavy frying pan, until hot but not smoking. Gently fry the sandwiches in batches for about 4–5 minutes until crisp and golden, turning once. Add more oil and butter as necessary. Drain on paper towels.

4 Transfer the sandwiches to a cutting board and cut each into 4 triangles, then each in half again. Make 64 triangles in total. Thread an olive and parsley leaf on to a cocktail stick, then stick into each triangle and serve at once while warm.

Potato Blinis

These light pancakes originate from Russia, where they are served with caviar. Here they are topped with cream and smoked salmon.

Serves 6

115g/4oz maincrop potatoes, boiled
   and mashed

15ml/1 tbsp easy-blend dried yeast

175g/6oz/1½ cups plain flour

oil, for greasing

90ml/6 tbsp soured cream

6 slices smoked salmon

salt and ground black pepper

lemon slices, to garnish

COOK'S TIP

These small pancakes can easily
be prepared in advance and
stored in the fridge until ready
for use. Simply warm them
through in a low oven.

1 In a large bowl, mix together the potatoes, dried yeast, flour and 300ml/½ pint/1¼ cups hand-hot water.

2 Leave to rise in a warm place for about 30 minutes until the mixture has doubled in size.

3 Heat a non-stick frying pan and add a little oil. Drop spoonfuls of the mixture on to the preheated pan. Cook the blinis for 2 minutes until lightly golden on the underside, toss with a spatula and cook on the second side for about 1 minute.

4 Season the blinis with some salt and pepper. Serve with a little soured cream and a small slice of smoked salmon folded on top. Garnish with a final grind of black pepper and a small slice of lemon.

Grilled Asparagus with Salt-cured Ham

Serve this tapas when asparagus is plentiful and not too expensive.

INGREDIENTS

Serves 4

6 slices of Serrano ham

12 asparagus spears

15ml/1 tbsp olive oil

sea salt and coarsely ground black pepper

COOK'S TIP

If you can't find Serrano ham, use Italian prosciutto or Portuguese presunto.

1 Preheat the grill to high. Halve each slice of ham lengthways and wrap one half around each of the asparagus spears.

2 Brush the ham and asparagus lightly with oil and sprinkle with salt and pepper. Place on the grill rack. Grill for 5–6 minutes, turning frequently, until the asparagus is tender but still firm. Serve immediately.

Dates Stuffed with Chorizo

This is a delicious combination from Spain, using fresh dates and spicy chorizo sausage.

INGREDIENTS

Serves 4–6

50g/2oz chorizo sausage

12 fresh dates, stoned

6 streaky bacon rashers

oil, for frying

plain flour, for dusting

1 egg, beaten

50g/2oz/1 cup fresh breadcrumbs

1 Trim the ends of the chorizo sausage and then peel away the skin. Cut into three 2cm/¾ in slices. Cut these in half lengthways, then into quarters, giving 12 pieces.

2 Stuff each date with a piece of chorizo, closing the date around it. Stretch the bacon, by running the back of a knife along the rasher. Cut each rasher in half, widthways. Wrap a piece of bacon around each date and secure with a wooden cocktail stick.

3 In a deep pan, heat 1cm/½ in of oil. Dust the dates with flour, dip them in the beaten egg, then coat in breadcrumbs. Fry the dates in the hot oil, turning them, until golden. Remove the dates with a draining spoon, and drain on kitchen paper. Serve at once.

Crispy Spring Rolls

These small and dainty spring rolls are ideal served as appetizers or as cocktail snacks. If liked, you could replace the mushrooms with chicken or pork and the carrots with prawns.

INGREDIENTS

Makes 40 rolls

225g/8oz fresh beansprouts

115g/4oz small leeks or spring onions

115g/4oz carrots

115g/4oz bamboo shoots, sliced

115g/4oz mushrooms

45–60ml/3–4 tbsp vegetable oil

5ml/1 tsp salt

5ml/1 tsp light brown sugar

15ml/1 tbsp light soy sauce

15ml/1 tbsp Chinese rice wine or
   dry sherry

20 frozen spring roll skins, defrosted

15ml/1 tbsp cornflour paste (see
   Cook's Tip)

flour, for dusting

oil, for deep-frying

1 Cut all the vegetables into thin shreds, roughly the same size and shape as the beansprouts.

2 Heat the oil in a wok and stir-fry the vegetables for about 1 minute. Add the salt, sugar, soy sauce and wine or sherry and continue stirring the vegetables for 1½–2 minutes. Remove and drain away the excess liquid, then leave to cool.

3 To make the spring rolls, cut each spring roll skin in half diagonally, then place about a tablespoonful of the vegetable mixture one-third of the way down on the skin, with the triangle pointing away from you.

COOK'S TIP

To make cornflour paste, mix together 4 parts cornflour with about 5 parts cold water until smooth.

4 Lift the lower edge over the filling and roll once.

5 Fold in both ends and roll once more, then brush the upper pointed edge with a little cornflour paste, and roll into a neat package. Lightly dust a tray with flour and place the spring rolls on the tray with the flapside underneath.

6 To cook, heat the oil in a wok or deep-fryer until hot, then reduce the heat to low. Deep-fry the spring rolls in batches (about 8–10 at a time) for 2–3 minutes or until golden and crispy, then remove and drain. Serve the spring rolls hot with a dipping sauce, such as soy sauce, or mixed salt and pepper.

Chorizo Pastry Puffs

These flaky pastry puffs, filled with spicy chorizo sausage and grated cheese, make a really superb accompaniment to a glass of cold sherry or beer. You can use any type of hard cheese for the puffs, but for best results, choose a mild variety, as the chorizo has plenty of flavour.

INGREDIENTS

Serves 8

225g/8oz puff pastry, thawed if frozen

115g/4oz cured chorizo sausage,
   finely chopped

50g/2oz/½ cup grated cheese

1 small egg, beaten

5ml/1 tsp paprika

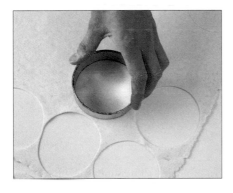

1 Roll out the pastry thinly on a floured work surface. Using a 7.5cm/3in cutter, stamp out as many rounds as possible, then re-roll the trimmings, if necessary, and stamp out more rounds to make 16 in all.

2 Preheat the oven to 230°C/450°F/Gas 8. Put the chopped chorizo sausage and grated cheese in a bowl and toss together lightly.

3 Lay one of the pastry rounds in the palm of your hand and place a little of the chorizo mixture across the centre.

4 Using your other hand, pinch the edges of the pastry together along the top to seal, as when making a miniature patty. Repeat the process with the remaining rounds to make 16 puffs in all.

5 Place the pastries on a nonstick baking sheet and brush lightly with the beaten egg. Using a small sifter or tea strainer, dust the tops lightly with a little of the paprika.

6 Bake the pastries in the oven for 10–12 minutes, until puffed and golden brown. Transfer the pastries to a wire rack. Leave to cool for 5 minutes, then serve the chorizo pastry puffs warm, dusted with the remaining paprika.

Samosas

These tasty party snacks are enjoyed the world over. Throughout the East, they are sold by street vendors, and eaten at any time of day. Filo pastry can be used if a lighter, flakier texture is preferred.

INGREDIENTS

Makes about 20

1 packet 25cm/10in square spring roll
    wrappers, thawed if frozen
30ml/2 tbsp plain flour, mixed to a paste
    with water
vegetable oil, for deep frying
coriander leaves, to garnish

For the filling

25g/1oz/2 tbsp ghee or unsalted butter
1 small onion finely chopped
1cm/½in piece fresh root ginger, peeled
    and chopped
1 garlic glove, crushed
2.5ml/½ tsp chilli powder
1 large potato, about 225g/8oz cooked
    until just tender and finely diced
50g/2oz/½ cup cauliflower florets, lightly
    cooked, chopped into small pieces
50g/2oz/½ cup frozen peas, thawed
5–10ml/1–2 tsp garam masala
15ml/1 tbsp chopped fresh coriander
    (leaves and stems)
squeeze of lemon juice
salt

1 Heat the ghee or butter in a large frying pan and fry the onion, ginger and garlic for 5 minutes until the onion has softened but not browned. Add the chilli powder and cook for 1 minute, then stir in the potato, cauliflower and peas. Sprinkle with garam masala and set aside to cool. Stir in the chopped coriander, lemon juice and salt.

2 Cut the spring roll wrappers into three strips (or two for larger samosas). Brush the edges with a little of the flour paste. Place a small spoonful of filling about 2cm/¾in in from the edge of one strip. Fold one corner over the filling to make a triangle and continue this folding until the entire strip has been used and a triangular pastry has been formed. Seal any open edges with more flour and water paste, if necessary adding more water if the paste is very thick.

3 Heat the oil for deep frying to 190°C/375°F and fry the samosas, a few at a time, until golden and crisp. Drain well on kitchen paper and serve hot garnished with coriander leaves.

COOK'S TIP

Prepare samosas in advance by frying until just cooked through and draining. Cook in hot oil for a few minutes to brown and drain again before serving

Rice Triangles

These rice shapes – Onigari – are very popular in Japan. You can put anything you like in the rice, so you could invent your own Onigiri.

Serves 4

1 salmon steak

15ml/1 tbsp salt

450g/1lb/4 cups freshly cooked sushi rice

¼ cucumber, seeded and cut into matchsticks

½ sheet yaki-nori seaweed, cut into four equal strips

white and black sesame seeds, for sprinkling

1 Grill the salmon steaks on each side , until the flesh flakes easily when tested with the tip of a sharp knife. Set aside to cool while you make other onigiri. When the salmon is cold, flake it, discarding any skin and bones.

2 Put the salt in a bowl. Spoon an eighth of the warm cooked rice into a small rice bowl. Make a hole in the middle of the rice and put in a few cucumber matchsticks. Smooth the rice over to cover.

3 Wet the palms of both hands with cold water, then rub the salt evenly on to your palms.

4 Empty the rice and cucumbers from the bowl onto one hand. Use both hands to shape the rice into a triangular shape, using firm but not heavy pressure, and making sure that the cucumber is encased by the rice. Make three more rice triangles the same way.

5 Mix the flaked salmon into the remaining rice, then shape it into triangles as before.

6 Wrap a strip of yaki- nori around each of the cucumber triangles. Sprinkle sesame seeds on the salmon triangles.

COOK'S TIP

Always use warm rice to make the triangles. Allow them to cool completely and wrap each in foil or clear film.

Mini Sausage Rolls

These miniature versions of old-fashioned sausage rolls are always popular – the Parmesan cheese gives them an extra special flavour.

INGREDIENTS

Makes about 48

15g/½ oz/1 tbsp butter

1 onion, finely chopped

350g/12oz good quality sausagemeat

15ml/1 tbsp dried mixed herbs such as oregano, thyme, sage, tarragon or dill

25g/1oz finely chopped pistachio nuts (optional)

350g/12oz puff pastry, thawed if frozen

60–90ml/4–6 tbsp freshly grated Parmesan cheese

salt and ground black pepper

1 egg, lightly beaten, for glazing

poppy seeds, sesame seeds, fennel seeds and aniseeds, for sprinkling

1 In a small frying pan, over a medium heat, melt the butter. Add the onion and cook for about 5 minutes, until softened. Remove from the heat and cool. Put the onion, sausagemeat, herbs, salt and pepper and nuts (if using) in a mixing bowl and stir together until completely blended.

2 Divide the sausage mixture into 4 equal portions and roll into thin sausages measuring about 25cm/10in long. Set aside.

3 On a lightly floured surface, roll out the pastry to about 3mm/⅛in thick. Cut the pastry into 4 strips 25 x 7.5cm/10 x 3in long. Place a long sausage on each pastry strip and sprinkle each with a little Parmesan cheese.

COOK'S TIP

Filo pastry can be used instead of puff pastry for a very light effect. Depending on the size of the filo sheets, cut into 8 pieces 25 x 7.5cm/10 x 3in. Brush 4 of the sheets with a little melted butter or vegetable oil and place a second pastry sheet on top. Place one sausage log on each of the four layered sheets and roll up and bake as above.

4 Brush one long edge of each of the pastry strips with the egg glaze and roll up to enclose each sausage. Set them seam-side down and press gently to seal. Brush each with the egg glaze and sprinkle with one type of seeds. Repeat with remaining pastry strips, using different seeds.

5 Preheat the oven to 220°C/425°F/Gas 7. Lightly grease a large baking sheet. Cut each of the pastry logs into 2.5cm/1in lengths and arrange on the baking sheet. Bake for about 15 minutes until the pastry is crisp and brown. Serve warm or allow to cool before serving.

Sushi-style Tuna Cubes

These tasty tuna cubes are easier to prepare than classic Japanese sushi but retain the same fresh taste.

Makes about 24

675g/1½ lb fresh tuna steak, about
   2cm/¾ in thick
1 large red pepper, seeded and cut into
   2cm/¾ in pieces
sesame seeds, for sprinkling

For the marinade
15–30ml/1–2 tbsp lemon juice
2.5ml/½ tsp salt
2.5ml/½ tsp sugar
2.5ml/½ tsp wasabi paste
120ml/4 fl oz/½ cup olive or vegetable oil
30ml/2 tbsp chopped fresh coriander

For the soy dipping sauce
105ml/7 tbsp soy sauce
15ml/1 tbsp rice wine vinegar
5ml/1 tsp lemon juice
1–2 spring onions, finely chopped
5ml/1 tsp sugar
2–3 dashes Asian hot chilli oil or hot
   pepper sauce

1 Cut the tuna into 2.5cm/1in pieces and then arrange them in a single layer in a large non-corrosive baking dish.

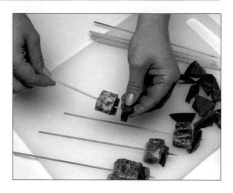

2 Prepare the marinade. In a small bowl, stir the lemon juice with the salt, sugar and wasabi paste. Slowly whisk in the oil until well blended and slightly creamy. Stir in the coriander. Pour over the tuna cubes and toss to coat. Cover and marinate for about 40 minutes in a cool place.

3 Meanwhile, prepare the soy dipping sauce. Combine all the ingredients in a small bowl and stir until well blended. Cover until ready to serve.

4 Preheat the grill and line a baking sheet with foil. Thread a cube of tuna then a piece of pepper on to each skewer and arrange on the baking sheet.

5 Sprinkle with sesame seeds and grill for 3–5 minutes, turning once or twice, until just beginning to colour but still pink inside. Serve with the soy dipping sauce.

COOK'S TIP

Wasabi is a hot, pungent Japanese horseradish available in powder form (that has to be reconstituted) and as paste in a tube from gourmet and Japanese food shops.

Lamb Tikka

Creamy yogurt and ground nuts go wonderfully with the spices in these little Indian meatballs.

INGREDIENTS

Makes about 20

450g/1lb lamb fillet

2 spring onions, chopped

For the marinade

350ml/12 fl oz/1½ cups natural yogurt

15ml/1 tbsp ground almonds, cashewnuts
  or peanuts

15ml/1 tbsp vegetable oil

2–3 garlic cloves, finely chopped

juice of 1 lemon

5ml/1 tsp garam masala or curry powder

2.5ml/½ tsp ground cardamom

1.5ml/¼ tsp cayenne pepper

15–30ml/1–2 tbsp chopped fresh mint

1 To prepare the marinade, stir together the marinade ingredients. In a separate small bowl, reserve about 120ml/4fl oz/½ cup of the mixture to use as a dipping sauce for the meatballs.

2 Cut the lamb into small pieces and put in the bowl of a food processor with the spring onions. Process, using the pulse action, until the meat is finely chopped. Add 30–45ml/2–3 tbsp of the marinade and process again.

4 With moistened palms, form the meat mixture into slightly oval-shaped balls, measuring about 4cm/1½in long, and arrange in a shallow baking dish. Spoon over the remaining marinade and chill the meatballs in the fridge for 8–10 hours or overnight.

3 Test to see if the mixture holds together by pinching a little between your fingertips. Add a little more marinade if necessary, but do not make the mixture too wet and soft.

5 Preheat the grill and line a baking sheet with foil. Thread each meatball on to a skewer and arrange on the baking sheet. Grill for 4–5 minutes, turning them occasionally, until crisp and golden on all sides. Serve with the reserved marinade as a dipping sauce.